The Great Omission

"There is NO one like Dallas. Finding more of his words is like getting hidden treasure. Read and grow!"

—John Ortberg, author of
God Is Closer Than You Think

"*The Great Omission* weaves together the themes developed in Willard's earlier writings and focuses them on the central point: a daily life of interactive apprenticeship to the Lord Jesus in the school of life. This is vintage Willard, and it must be read by all who hunger to grow as Jesus's disciple."

—J. P. Moreland, Distinguished Professor of
Philosophy, Talbot School of Theology, and
author of *Love Your God with All Your Mind*

"I know no one like Dallas Willard who can express profound things so simply and simple things so profoundly. I never fail to benefit from his writings."

—Os Guinness, author of *The Call and Unspeakable*

"Dallas Willard reminds us that a relationship with Jesus only makes sense when we choose to become his apprentices."

—Alan Andrews, U.S. President of the Navigators

THE GREAT OMISSION

THE GREAT OMISSION

Reclaiming Jesus's Essential
Teachings on Discipleship

DALLAS WILLARD

HarperOne
An Imprint of HarperCollins*Publishers*

HarperOne

Credits and permissions begin on page 235, which constitutes a continuation of this copyright page.

THE GREAT OMISSION: *Reclaiming Jesus's Essential Teachings on Discipleship.* Copyright © 2006 by Dallas Willard. All rights reserved. Printed in the United States of America. No part of this book may be used or reproduced in any manner whatsoever without written permission except in the case of brief quotations embodied in critical articles and reviews. For information address HarperCollins Publishers, 195 Broadway, New York, NY 10007.

HarperCollins books may be purchased for educational, business, or sales promotional use. For information please e-mail the Special Markets Department at SPsales@harpercollins.com.

HarperCollins website: http://www.harpercollins.com

HarperCollins®, 📖®, and HarperOne™ are trademarks of HarperCollins Publishers

FIRST HARPERCOLLINS PAPERBACK EDITION PUBLISHED IN 2014

Library of Congress Cataloging-in-Publication Data
Willard, Dallas.
    The great omission : reclaiming Jesus's essential teachings on discipleship /
Dallas Willard.—1st ed.
    p.   cm.
ISBN: 978–0–06–231175–7
    1. Christian life.   2. Spiritual formation.   3. Jesus Christ—Teachings.   I. Title.
BS2417.C5W55   2006
248.4—dc22   2006040052

23 24 25 26 27 LBC 13 12 11 10 9

To

BERTHA VONALLMAN WILLARD

A true apprentice of Jesus
Who has blessed all she has touched—
Grace and truth through and through

CONTENTS

Discipleship of the Soul and the Mind

Books on Spiritual Living: Visions and Practices

INTRODUCTION

Joy to the world, the Lord is come, let Earth receive her King! Let every heart, prepare him room, and heaven and nature sing!" So sings the grand old Christmas carol, with the implication that now, with the coming of Jesus into our world and our lives, things are going to be *really different*. And that theme is sustained through the ages up to the present. No knowledgeable person can think anything else. Transformation into goodness is what the "Good News" is all about . . . isn't it?

But there is a great deal of disappointment expressed today about the character and the effects of Christian people, about Christian institutions, and—at least by implication—about the Christian faith and understanding of reality. Most of the disappointment comes from Christians themselves, who find that what they profess "just isn't working"—not for themselves nor, so far as they can see, for those around them. What *they* have found, at least, does not "exceed all expectations," as the standard evaluation form says. "Disappointment" books form a subcategory of Christian publishing. Self-flagellation has not disappeared from the Christian repertoire.

But the disappointment also comes from those who merely stand apart from "visible" Christianity (perhaps they have no real knowledge of the situation, or have just "had enough"), as well as from those who openly oppose it. These people often beat Christians with their own stick, criticizing them in terms that Jesus himself provides. There is an obvious Great Disparity between, on the one hand, the *hope for life expressed in Jesus*—found real in the Bible and in many shining examples from among his followers—and, on the other hand, the *actual day-to-day behavior, inner life, and social presence* of most of those who now profess adherence to him.

The question must arise: Why the Great Disparity? Is it caused by something built into the very nature of Jesus and what he taught and brought to humankind? Or is it the result of inessential factors that attach themselves to Christian institutions and people as they journey through time? Are we in a period when both rank-and-file Christians and most of their leaders have, for some reason, missed the main point?

If your neighbor is having trouble with his automobile, you might think he just got a lemon. And you might be right. But if you found that he was supplementing his gasoline with a quart of water now and then, you would not blame the car or its maker for it not running, or for running in fits and starts. You would say that the car was not built to work under the conditions imposed by the owner. And you would certainly advise him to put only the appropriate kind of fuel in the tank. After some restorative work, perhaps the car would then run fine.

We must approach current disappointments about the walk with Christ in a similar way. It too is not meant to run on just anything you may give it. If it doesn't work at all, or only in fits and starts, that is because *we do not give ourselves to it in a way that allows our lives to be taken over by it.* Perhaps we have never been told what to do. We are misinformed about "our part" in eternal living. Or we have just learned the "faith and practice" of some group we have fallen in with, not that of Jesus himself. Or maybe we have heard something that is right-on with Jesus himself, but misunderstood it (a dilemma that tends to produce good Pharisees or "legalists," which is a really hard life.) Or perhaps we thought the "Way" we have heard of seemed too costly and we have tried to economize (supplying a quart of moralistic or religious "water" now and then).

Now we know that the "car" of Christianity can run, and run gloriously, in every kind of external circumstance. We have seen it—or at least, anyone who wishes to can see it—merely by looking, past the caricatures and partial presentations, at Jesus himself and at the many manifestations of him in events and personalities throughout history and in our world today. He is, simply, the brightest spot in the human scene. There is no real competition. Even anti-Christians judge and condemn Christians in terms of Jesus and what he said. He is not really *hidden.* But for all his manifest presence in our world, he must be sought. That is part of his plan, and for our benefit. If we do seek him, he will certainly find us, and then we, ever more deeply, find him. That is the blessed existence of the *disciple of Jesus* who continuously "grows in the grace and knowledge of our Lord and Savior Jesus Christ" (2 Peter 3:18).

But just there is the problem. Who, among Christians today, is a disciple of Jesus, in any substantive sense of the word "disciple"? A disciple is a learner, a student, an apprentice—a *practitioner,* even if only a beginner. The New Testament literature, which must be allowed to define our terms if we are ever to get our bearings in the Way with Christ, makes this clear. In that context, disciples of Jesus are people who do not just profess certain views as their own but apply their growing understanding of life in the Kingdom of the Heavens to every aspect of their life on earth.

In contrast, the governing assumption today, among professing Christians, is that we can be "Christians" forever and never become disciples. Not even in heaven, it seems, for who would need it there? That is the accepted teaching now. Check it out wherever you are. And this (with its various consequences) is the Great Omission from the "Great Commission" in which the Great Disparity is firmly rooted. As long as the Great Omission is permitted or sustained, the Great Disparity will flourish—in individual lives as well as in Christian groups and movements. Conversely, if we cut the root in the Great Omission, the Great Disparity will wither, as it has repeatedly done in times past. No need to fight it. Just stop feeding it.

Jesus told us explicitly what to do. We have a manual, just like the car owner. He told us, *as* disciples, to *make disciples*. Not converts to Christianity, nor to some particular "faith and practice." He did not tell us to arrange for people to "get in" or "make the cut" after they die, nor to eliminate the various brutal forms of injustice, nor to produce and maintain "successful" churches. These are all good things, and he had something to say about all of them. They will certainly happen if—but *only if*—we are (his constant apprentices) and do (make constant apprentices) what he told us to be and do. If we just do this, it will little matter what else we do or do not do.

Once we who are disciples have assisted others with becoming disciples (of Jesus, *not* of us), we can gather them, in ordinary life situations, under the supernatural Trinitarian Presence, forming a new kind of social unit never before seen on earth. These disciples are his "called-out" ones, his *ecclesia*. Their "walk" is already "in heaven" (Philippians 3:20), because heaven is in action where they are (Ephesians 2:6). Now it is *these* people who can be taught "to observe all things whatsoever I have commanded you." In becoming his students or apprentices, they have agreed to be taught, and the resources are available, so they can methodically go about doing it. This reliably yields the life that proves to "exceed all expectations."

Jesus put it this way to his little group of immediate followers: "I have been given say over all things in heaven and in the earth. As you go, therefore, make disciples of all kinds of people, submerge them in Trinitarian Presence, and show them how to do everything I have commanded. And now look: I am with you every minute until the job is done" (Matthew 28:18–20). We see in world history the results of a small number of his disciples simply doing what he said, with no "Omission."

People in Western churches, and especially in North America, usually assume without thinking that the Great Commission of Jesus is something to be carried out in *other* countries. This is caused in part by the use of "nations" to translate ἔθνη, when a better translation might be our contemporary "ethnic groups," or just "people of every kind." But this leads in practice to *not* treating "our kind of people" as the ones to be led into discipleship to Jesus. Some actually think that "we" don't need it, because *we* are basically right to begin with. But in fact the primary mission field for the Great Commission today is made up of the churches in Europe and North America. That is where the Great Disparity is most visible, and from where it threatens to spread to the rest of the world. Our responsibility is to implement the Great Commission right where we are, not just to raise efforts to do it elsewhere. And if we don't, it won't even be implemented "over there."

It is a tragic error to think that Jesus was telling us, as he left, to start churches, as that is understood today. From time to time starting a church may be appropriate. But his aim for us is much greater than that. He wants us to establish "beachheads" or bases of operation for the Kingdom of God wherever we are. In this way God's promise to Abraham—that in him and in his seed all peoples of the earth would be blessed (Genesis 12:3)—is carried forward toward its realization. The outward effect of this life in

Christ is *perpetual moral revolution, until the purpose of humanity on earth is completed.*

This vision of the meaning of world history is explained in detail in the general introduction to the *Renovaré Spiritual Formation Bible* (2005). As disciples of Jesus, we today are a part of God's world project. But realization of that project, it must never be forgotten, is the effect, not the life itself. The *mission* naturally flows from the *life*. It is not an afterthought, or something we might overlook or omit as we live the life. The eternal life, from which many profound and glorious effects flow, is *interactive relationship with God and with his special Son, Jesus, within the abiding ambience of the Holy Spirit.* Eternal life is the Kingdom Walk, where, in seamless unity, we "Do justice, love kindness, and walk carefully with our God" (Micah 6:8). We learn to walk this way through apprenticeship to Jesus. His school is always in session

We need to emphasize that the Great Omission from the Great Commission is *not* obedience to Christ, but discipleship, apprenticeship, to him. Through discipleship, obedience will take care of itself, and we will also escape the snares of judgmentalism and legalism, whether directed toward ourselves or toward others.

Now, some might be shocked to hear that what the "church"—the disciples gathered—really needs is not more people, more money, better buildings or programs, more education, or more prestige. Christ's gathered people, the church, has always been at its best when it had little or none of these. All it needs to fulfill Christ's purposes on earth is *the quality of life he makes real in the life of his disciples.* Given that quality, the church will prosper from everything that comes its way as it makes clear and available on earth the "life that is life indeed." There will always be many battles to fight, but the brooding presence of the Great Disparity, and the illusion that *it* is all that Christ has to offer humanity, will not be one of them.

So the greatest issue facing the world today, with all its heart-breaking needs, is whether those who, by profession or culture, are identified as "Christians" will become *disciples*— students, apprentices, practitioners—*of Jesus Christ,* steadily learning from him how to live the life of the Kingdom of the Heavens into every corner of human existence. Will they break out of the churches to be his Church—to be, without human force or violence, his mighty force for good on earth, drawing the churches after them toward the eternal purposes of God? And, on its own scale, there is no greater issue facing the individual human being, Christian or not.

Can anything be said to help us make the transitions into and within discipleship to Jesus Christ? The pages that follow contain several previously published articles and addresses on discipleship, spiritual disciplines, and spiritual growth and formation. They are now almost impossible for the ordinary person to find, but some have thought that there is a real need for them to be available. Some of the selections have been revised in minor ways, but they are all presented here substantially as they were originally published or given. There is some small degree of repetition, since they are "occasional" pieces, and some variations of style. Some are explicitly addressed to ministers, but the principles in them apply to everyone. I hope this will not prove to be a distraction. I have attached a final "Parting Word" in which I try to emphasize the simplicity of the "next steps" that can orient individuals and groups for action.

What Jesus expects us to do is not complicated or obscure. In some cases, it will require that we change what we have been doing. But the Great Commission—*his* plan for spiritual formation, "church growth," and world service—is pretty obvious. Let's just do it. He will provide all the teaching and support we need. Remember, "when all else fails, follow the instructions."

APPRENTICED TO JESUS

CHAPTER 1

Discipleship

For Super Christians Only?

THE WORD "DISCIPLE" occurs 269 times in the New Testament. "Christian" is found three times and was first introduced to refer precisely to disciples of Jesus—in a situation where it was no longer possible to regard them as a sect of the Jews (Acts 11:26). The New Testament is a book about disciples, by disciples, and for disciples of Jesus Christ.

But the point is not merely verbal. What is more important is that the kind of life we see in the earliest church is that of a special type of person. All of the assurances and benefits offered to humankind in the gospel evidently presuppose such a life and do not make realistic sense apart from it. The disciple of Jesus is not the deluxe or heavy-duty model of the Christian—especially padded, textured, streamlined, and empowered for the fast lane on the straight and narrow way. He or she stands on the pages of the New Testament as the first level of basic transportation in the Kingdom of God.

Undiscipled Disciples

For at least several decades the churches of the Western world have not made discipleship a condition of being a Christian. One is not required to be, or to intend to be, a disciple in order to become a Christian, and one may remain a Christian without any signs of progress toward or in discipleship. Contemporary American churches in particular do not require following Christ in his example, spirit, and teachings as a condition of membership—either of entering into or continuing in fellowship of a denomination or local church. I would be glad to learn of any exception to this claim, but it would only serve to highlight its general validity and make the general rule more glaring. So far as the visible Christian institutions of our day are concerned, *discipleship clearly is optional.*

That, of course, is no secret. The best of current literature on discipleship either states outright or assumes that the Christian may not be a disciple at all—even after a lifetime as a church member. A widely used book, *The Lost Art of Disciple Making,* presents the Christian life on three possible levels: the convert, the disciple, and the worker. There is a process for bringing persons to each level, it states. Evangelizing produces converts, establishing or "follow-up" produces disciples, and equipping produces workers. Disciples and workers are said to be able to renew the cycle by evangelizing, while only workers can make disciples through follow-up.

The picture of "church life" presented by this book conforms generally to American Christian practice. But does that model not make discipleship something entirely optional? Clearly it does, just as whether the disciple will become a "worker" is an option. Vast numbers of converts today thus exercise the options permitted by the message they hear: they choose not to become—or at least do not choose to become—disciples of Jesus Christ. Churches are filled with "undiscipled disciples," as Jess Moody has called them.

Of course there is in reality no such thing. Most problems in contemporary churches can be explained by the fact that members have never decided to follow Christ.

In this situation, little good results from insisting that Christ is *also supposed to be* Lord. To present his Lordship as an option leaves it squarely in the category of the special wheels, tires, and stereo equipment. You can do without it. And it is—alas!—far from clear what you would do with it. Obedience and training in obedience form no intelligible doctrinal or practical unity with the "salvation" presented in recent versions of the gospel.

Great Omissions from the Great Commission

A different model of life was instituted in the "Great Commission" Jesus left for his people. The first goal he set for the early church was to use his all-encompassing power and authority to make disciples without regard to ethnic distinctions—from all "nations" (Matthew 28:19). That made clear a world-historical project and set aside his earlier strategic directive to go only to "the lost sheep of the house of Israel" (Matthew 10:6). Having made disciples, these alone were to be baptized into the name of the Father, and of the Son, and of the Holy Spirit. Given this twofold preparation, they were then to be taught to treasure and keep "all things whatsoever I have commanded you" (Matthew 28:20). The Christian church of the first centuries resulted from following this plan for church growth—a result hard to improve upon.

But in place of Christ's plan, historical drift has substituted "Make converts (to a particular 'faith and practice') and baptize them into church membership." This causes two great omissions from the Great Commission to stand out. Most important, we start by omitting the making of disciples and enrolling people as Christ's students, when we should let all else wait for that. Then we also omit, of necessity, the step of taking our converts through training that will bring them ever-increasingly to do what Jesus directed.

These two great omissions are connected in practice into one whole. Not having made our converts disciples, it is *impossible* for us to teach them how to live as Christ lived and taught (Luke 14:26). That was not a part of the package, not what they converted *to*. When confronted with the example and teachings of Christ, the response today is less one of rebellion or rejection than one of puzzlement: How do we relate to these? What have they to do with us? Isn't this bait and switch?

Discipleship Then

When Jesus walked among humankind there was a certain simplicity to being his disciple. Primarily it meant to go with him, in an attitude of observation, study, obedience, and imitation. There were no correspondence courses. One knew what to do and what it would cost. Simon Peter exclaimed, "Look, we have left everything and followed you" (Mark 10:28). Family and occupations were deserted for long periods to go with Jesus as he walked from place to place announcing, showing, and explaining the here-and-now governance or action of God. Disciples had to be with him to learn how to do what he did.

Imagine doing that today. How would family members, employers, and co-workers react to such abandonment? Probably they would conclude that we did not much care for them, or even for ourselves. Did not Zebedee think this as he watched his two sons desert the family business to keep company with Jesus (Mark 1:20)? Ask any father in a similar situation. So when Jesus observed that one must forsake the dearest things—family, "all that he hath," and "his own life also" (Luke 14:26, 33)—insofar as that was necessary to accompany him, he stated a simple fact: it was the only possible doorway to discipleship.

Discipleship Now

Though costly, discipleship once had a very clear, straightforward meaning. The mechanics are not the same today. We cannot literally be with him in the same way as his first disciples could. But the priorities and intentions—the heart or inner attitudes—of disciples are forever the same. In the heart of a disciple there is a *desire*, and there is a *decision* or settled intent. Having come to some understanding of what it means, and thus having "counted up the costs," the disciple of Christ desires above all else to be like him. Thus, "it is enough for the disciple to be like the teacher" (Matthew 10:25). And moreover, "everyone who is fully qualified will be like the teacher" (Luke 6:40).

Given this desire, usually produced by the lives and words of those already in the Way, there is still a decision to be made: the decision to devote oneself to becoming like Christ. The disciple is one who, intent upon becoming Christ-like and so dwelling in *his* "faith and practice," systematically and progressively rearranges his affairs to that end. By these decisions and actions, even today, one enrolls in Christ's training, becomes his pupil or disciple. There is no other way. We must keep this in mind should we, as disciples, decide to *make disciples*.

In contrast, the nondisciple, whether inside or outside the church, has something "more important" to do or undertake than to become like Jesus Christ. He or she has "bought a piece of ground," perhaps, or even five yoke of oxen, or has taken a spouse (Luke 14:18, 19). Such lame excuses only reveal that something on that dreary list of security, reputation, wealth, power, sensual indulgence, or mere distraction and numbness, still retains his or her ultimate allegiance. Or if someone has seen through these, he or she may not know the alternative—not know, especially, that it is *possible* to live under the care and governance of God, working and living with Him as Jesus did, always "seeking first the kingdom of God and his righteousness."

A mind cluttered by excuses may make a mystery of discipleship, or it may see it as something to be dreaded. But there is no mystery about desiring and intending to be like someone—that is a very common thing. And if we really do intend to be like Christ, that will be obvious to every thoughtful person around us, as well as to ourselves. Of course, attitudes that define the disciple cannot be realized today by leaving family and business to accompany Jesus on his travels about the countryside. But discipleship can be made concrete by actively learning how to love our enemies, bless those who curse us, walk the second mile with an oppressor—in general, living out the gracious inward transformations of faith, hope, and love. Such acts—carried out by the disciplined person with manifest grace, peace, and joy—make discipleship no less tangible and shocking today than were those desertions of long ago. Anyone who will enter into the Way can verify this, and he or she will at the same time prove that discipleship is far from dreadful.

The Cost of Nondiscipleship

In 1937 Dietrich Bonhoeffer gave the world his book *The Cost of Discipleship*.[1] It was a masterful attack on "easy Christianity" or "cheap grace," in the context of mid-twentieth-century Europe and America. But it did not succeed in setting aside—perhaps it even enforced—the view of discipleship as a costly spiritual excess, and only for those especially driven or called to it. It was right and good of Bonhoeffer to point out that one cannot be a disciple of Christ without forfeiting things normally sought in human life, and that one who pays little in the world's coinage to bear his name has reason to wonder where he or she stands with God. But the cost of *non*discipleship is far greater—even when this life alone is considered—than the price paid to walk with Jesus, constantly learning from him.

Nondiscipleship costs abiding peace, a life penetrated throughout by love, faith that sees everything in the light of God's overriding governance for good, hopefulness that stands firm in the most discouraging of circumstances, power to do what is right and withstand the forces of evil. In short, nondiscipleship costs you exactly that abundance of life Jesus said he came to bring (John 10:10). The cross-shaped yoke of Christ is after all an instrument of liberation and power to those who live in it with him and learn the meekness and lowliness of heart that brings rest to the soul.

"Follow Me. I'm Found!"

Leo Tolstoy wrote that "man's whole life is a continual contradiction of what he knows to be his duty. In every department of life he acts in defiant opposition to the dictates of his conscience and his common sense."[2] In our age of bumper-sticker communications, some clever entrepreneur has devised a frame for the rear license plate that advises, "Don't follow me. I'm lost." It has had amazingly wide use, possibly because it touches with a little humor upon the universal failure referred to by Tolstoy. This failure causes a pervasive and profound hopelessness and sense of worthlessness: a sense that I could never stand in my world as a salty, light-giving example, showing people the Way of Life. Jesus's description of savorless salt sadly serves well to characterize how we feel about ourselves: "no longer good for anything, but [to be] thrown out and trampled under foot" (Matthew 5:13), and not even fit to mollify a manure pile (Luke 14:35).

A common saying expresses the same attitude: "Don't do as I do, do as I say" (more laughs?). Jesus said of certain religious leaders—the scribes and Pharisees—of his day, "Do whatever they teach you and follow it; but do not do as they do, for they do not practice what they teach" (Matthew 23:3). But that was no joke, and still isn't. We must ask what he would say of us today. Have we not elevated this practice of the scribes and Pharisees into a first principle of the Christian life? Is that not the effect, whether intended or not, of making discipleship optional?

We are not speaking here of *perfection,* nor of *earning* God's gift of life. Our concern is only with the manner of *entering into* that life. While none can merit salvation, or the fullness of life of which it is the root and natural part, all must act if it is to be theirs. By what actions of the heart, what desires and intentions, do we find access to life in Christ? Paul's example instructs us. He could say, in almost one breath, both "I am not perfect" (Philippians 3:12) and "Do what I do" (Philippians 4:9). His shortcomings—whatever they were—lay back of him, but he lived forward into the future through his intention to attain to Christ. He was both intent upon being like Christ (Philippians 3:10–14) and confident of upholding grace for his intention. He could thus say to all, "Follow me. I'm found!" ("Be imitators of me, as I am of Christ"—1 Corinthians 11:1).

Life's Greatest Opportunity

Dr. Rufus Jones has reflected in a recent book upon how little impact the twentieth-century evangelical church has had on societal problems. He attributes the deficiency to a corresponding lack of concern for social justice on the part of conservatives. That, in turn, is traced to reactions against liberal theology, deriving from the fundamentalist/modernist controversy of past decades. These are points we must take very seriously.

Causal connections in society and history are hard to trace, but I believe this is an inadequate diagnosis. After all, the lack of concern for social justice, where that is evident, itself requires an explanation. And the current position of the church in our world may be better explained by *what liberals and conservatives have shared* than by how they differ. For different reasons, and with different emphases, they have agreed that discipleship to Christ is optional to membership in the Christian church. Thus, the very type of life that could change the course of human society—and upon occasion has done so—is excluded or at least omitted from the essential message of the church.

Concerned to enter that radiant life we each must ask, "Am I a disciple, or only a Christian by current standards?" Examination of our ultimate desires and intentions, reflected in the specific responses and choices that make up our lives, can show whether there are things we hold more important than being like him. If there are, then we are not yet his disciples. Being unwilling to follow him, our claim of trusting him must ring hollow. We could never credibly claim to trust a doctor, teacher, or auto mechanic whose directions we would not follow.

For those who lead or minister, there are yet graver questions: What authority or basis do I have to baptize people who have not been brought to a clear decision to be a disciple of Christ? Dare I tell people, as "believers" without discipleship, that they are at peace with God and God with them? Where can I find justification for such a message? Perhaps most important: Do I as a minister have the faith to undertake the work of disciple-making? Is my first aim to make disciples? Or do I just run an operation?

Nothing less than life in the steps of Christ is adequate to the human soul or the needs of our world. Any other offer fails to do justice to the drama of human redemption, deprives the hearer of life's greatest opportunity, and abandons this present life to the

evil powers of the age. The correct perspective is to see following Christ not only as the necessity it is, but as the fulfillment of
the highest human possibilities and as life on the highest plane. It
is to see, in Helmut Thielicke's words, that "the Christian stands,
not under the dictatorship of a legalistic 'You ought,' but in the
magnetic field of Christian freedom, under the empowering of the
'You may.'"

CHAPTER 2

Why Bother with Discipleship?

I F WE ARE CHRISTIANS simply by believing that Jesus died for our sins, then that is all it takes to have sins forgiven and go to heaven when we die. Why, then, do some people keep insisting that something more than this is desirable? Lordship, discipleship, spiritual formation, and the like?

What more could one want than to be sure of one's eternal destiny and to enjoy life among others who profess the same faith? Of course everyone wants to be a good person. But that does not require that you actually *do* what Jesus himself said and did. Haven't you heard? "Christians aren't perfect, just forgiven."

Now, those who honestly find themselves concerned about such matters might find it helpful to consider four simple points:

First, there is absolutely nothing in what Jesus himself or his early followers taught that suggests you can *decide* just to enjoy forgiveness at Jesus's expense and have nothing more to do with him.

Some years ago A. W. Tozer expressed his "feeling that a notable heresy has come into being throughout evangelical Christian circles—the widely accepted concept that we humans can choose to accept Christ only because we need him as Savior and that we have the right to postpone our obedience to him as Lord as long as we want to!"[1] He then goes on to state "that salvation apart from obedience is unknown in the sacred scriptures."

This "heresy" has created the impression that it is quite reasonable to be a "vampire Christian." One in effect says to Jesus, "I'd like a little of your blood, please. But I don't care to be your student or have your character. In fact, won't you just excuse me while I get on with my life, and I'll see you in heaven." But can we really imagine that this is an approach that Jesus finds acceptable?

And when you stop to think about it, how could one actually trust him for forgiveness of sins while not trusting him for much more than that? You can't trust *him* without believing that he was right about everything, and that he alone has the key to every aspect of our lives here on earth. But if you believe *that,* you will naturally want to stay just as close to him as you can, in every aspect of your life.

Second, if we do not become his apprentices in Kingdom living, we remain locked in defeat so far as our moral intentions are concerned. This is where most professing Christians find themselves today. Statistical studies prove it. People, generally, choose to sin. And they are filled with explanations as to why, everything considered, it is "necessary" to do so. But, even so, no one wants to be *a sinner.* It is amusing that people will admit to lying, for example, but stoutly deny that they are liars.

We want to be good, but we are prepared, ready, to do evil— should circumstances *require* it. And of course they do "require" it, with deadening regularity. As Jesus himself indicated, those who practice sin actually are slaves of it (John 8:34). Ordinary life confirms it. How consistently do you find people who routinely succeed in doing the good and avoiding the evil they intend?

In contrast, *practicing* Jesus's words, as his apprentices, enables us to understand our lives and to see how we can interact with God's redemptive resources, ever at hand. This in turn gives us an increasing freedom from failed intentions as we learn from him how to, simply, *do what we know to be right.* By a practiced abiding in his words, we come to know the truth, and the truth does, sure enough, make us free (John 8:36). We are able to do the good we intend.

Third, only avid discipleship to Christ through the Spirit brings the inward transformation of thought, feeling, and character that "cleans the inside of the cup" (Matthew 23:25) and "makes the tree good" (Matthew 12:33). As we study with Jesus we increasingly become on the inside—with the "Father who is in secret" (Matthew 6:6)—exactly what we are on the outside, where actions and moods and attitudes visibly play over our body, alive in its social context. An amazing simplicity will take over our lives—a simplicity that is *really* just transparency.

This requires a long and careful learning from Jesus to remove the *duplicity* that has become second nature to us—as is perhaps inevitable in a world where, to "manage" our relations to those about us, we must hide what we really think, feel, and would like to do, if only we could avoid observation. Thus, a part of Jesus's teaching was to "avoid the leaven, or permeating spirit, of the Pharisees, which is hypocrisy" (Luke 12:1).

The Pharisees were in many respects the very best people of Jesus's day. But they located goodness in behavior and tried to secure themselves by careful management at the behavioral level. However, that simply cannot be done. Behavior is driven by the hidden or secret dimension of human personality, from the depths of the soul and body, and what is present there *will* escape. Hence, the Pharisee always fails at some point to do what is right, and then must redefine, redescribe, or explain it away—or simply hide it.

In contrast, the *fruit* of the spirit, as described by Jesus, Paul, and other biblical writers, does not consist in actions, but in attitudes or settled personality traits that make up the substance of the "hidden" self, the "inner man." "Love" captures this fruit in one word, but does so in such a concentrated form that it needs to be spelled out. Thus, the "fruit [singular] of the Spirit is love, joy, peace, patience, kindness, generosity, faithfulness, gentleness, and self-control" (Galatians 5:22). Other such passages easily come to mind, such as 2 Peter 1:4–8, 1 Corinthians 13, and Romans 5:1–5.

"Spiritual formation" in the Christian tradition is a process of increasingly being possessed and permeated by such character traits as we walk in the easy yoke of discipleship with Jesus our teacher. From the inward character the deeds of love then naturally—but supernaturally—and transparently flow. Of course there will always be room for improvement, so we need not worry that we will become perfect—at least for a few weeks or months. Our aim is to be pervasively possessed by Jesus through constant companionship with him. Like our brother Paul, "This one thing I do: . . . I press on toward the goal! . . . That I may know Christ!" (Philippians 3:13–14, 8).

Finally, for the one who makes sure to walk as close to Jesus as possible there comes the reliable exercise of a power that is beyond them in dealing with the problems and evils that afflict earthly existence. Jesus is actually looking for people he can trust with his power. He knows that otherwise we remain largely helpless in the face of the organized and disorganized evils around us, and that we are unable—given his chosen strategy—to promote his will for good in this world with adequate power.

He is the one who said, "I have been given say over all things in heaven and earth. So you go . . ." (Matthew 28:18). Of him it was said that "God anointed Jesus of Nazareth with the Holy Ghost and with power, and he went about doing good, and healing all that were oppressed of the devil; *for God was with him*" (Acts 10:38). It is also given to us, we are called, to do his work by his power and not our own.

However we may understand the details, there can be no doubt, on the biblical picture of human life, that we were meant to be inhabited by God and to live by a power beyond ourselves. Human problems cannot be solved by human means. Human life can never flourish unless it pulses with the "immeasurable greatness of his power for us who believe" (Ephesians 1:19). But only constant students of Jesus will be given adequate power to fulfill their calling to be God's person for their time and their place in this world. They are the only ones who develop the character which makes it safe to have such power.

But, someone will say, can I not be "saved"—that is, get into heaven when I die—without any of this? Perhaps you can. God's goodness is so great, I am sure that He will let you in if He can find any basis at all to do so. But you might wish to think about what your life amounts to *before* you die, about what kind of person you are becoming, and about whether you really would be comfortable for eternity in the presence of One whose company you have not found especially desirable for the few hours and days of your earthly existence. And He is, after all, One who says to you *now*, "Follow me!"

CHAPTER 3

Who Is Your Teacher?

ODAY IS OFTEN SPOKEN OF as the age of information.
Information is vital to all we do of course, but then it
always has been. What distinguishes the present time is
that there is a lot more information (and misinformation) available than ever before, and a lot of people are trying to sell it to us.

What happens to Jesus in the crush of the information pushers? Unfortunately, he is usually pushed aside. Many Christians do not even think of him as one with reliable information about their lives. Consequently they do not become his students. What does he have to teach them? It is very common to find Christians who work hard to master a profession and succeed very well in human estimation, while the content of their studies contains no reference at all to Jesus or his teaching. How could this be?

A short while ago I led a faculty retreat for one of the better Christian colleges in the United States. In opening my presentation, I told the group that the important question to consider was what Jesus himself would say to them if he were the speaker at their retreat. I indicated my conviction that he would ask them this simple question: Why don't you respect me in your various fields of study and expertise? Why don't you recognize me as master of research and knowledge in your fields?

The response of these Christian professionals was interesting to observe, to say the least. Some thought the question would be entirely appropriate. Many were unsure of exactly what I was saying. Quite a number responded with, "Are you serious?" The idea that Jesus is master of fields such as algebra, economics, business administration, or French literature simply had not crossed their minds—and had a hard time finding access when presented to them.

That brings out a profoundly significant fact. In our culture, and among Christians as well, Jesus Christ is automatically disassociated from brilliance or intellectual capacity. Not one in a thousand will spontaneously think of him in conjunction with words such as "well informed," "brilliant," or "smart."

Far too often he is regarded as hardly conscious. He is taken as a mere icon, a wraithlike semblance of a man living on the margins of the "real life" where you and I must dwell. He is perhaps fit for the role of sacrificial lamb or alienated social critic, but little more.

But can we seriously imagine that Jesus could be Lord if he were not smart? If he were divine, would he be dumb? Or uninformed? Once you stop to think about it, how could he be what Christians take him to be in other respects and not be the best informed and most intelligent person of all—the smartest person who ever lived, bringing us the best information on the most important subjects?

What lies at the heart of the astonishing disregard of Jesus found in the moment-to-moment existence of multitudes of professing Christians is a simple *lack of respect for him.* He is not seriously taken to be a person of great ability. But how, then, can we *admire* him? And what can devotion or worship mean if simple respect is not included in it?

In contrast, the early Christians, who took the power of God's life in Jesus to all quarters of the earth, thought of Jesus as one "in whom are hidden all the treasures of wisdom and knowledge" (Colossians 2:3). They thought of him as master of every domain of life.

A natural progression of this confidence in him was toward doing everything, "in word or deed, . . . in the name of the Lord Jesus, giving thanks to God the Father through him" (Colossians 3:17). That is, they learned to do everything they said or did in cooperative action with Jesus, their always present teacher.

If we would live the life which God made us for, we must take our guiding information from Jesus in three respects:

First, we must learn from him the reason why we live and why we do the things we do. Here as elsewhere we are constantly bombarded by misinformation that leaves us to be manipulated into misery by our own desires and the will of those who would use us. The usual human fate is to choose a job, a profession, a spouse, or a house, only for one's own greater pleasure, power, and glory. Here rules "the lust of the flesh, the lust of the eyes, and the pride of life" (1 John 2:16), shattering life as it goes.

Jesus brings us reliable information about who we are, why we are here, and what the humanly appropriate motives are for doing whatever we do. First, he informs us that we are by nature unceasing spiritual beings with an eternal destiny in God's great universe. We will never stop existing, and there is nothing we can do about it.

While we have already fallen from God's intentions for us, he can restore us into the flow of God's life if we will only count on him for everything. That is, we must trust him, and really to trust him is to take up his cause, his "yoke" (Matthew 11:29). Then he will teach us how to make our choices with the aim of glorifying God by doing good to human beings. Under his instruction, this will prove to be the most exhilarating kind of life imaginable, with a scope and richness of personal creativity that never stops increasing.

Second, we must learn from Jesus, our "in-former," a new internal character: new "bowels," one old translation says. New *guts* we should frankly say today (see also Colossians 3:9–10). He teaches us in the first place that this is what God intends for us, and what he makes possible.

The central teachings of Jesus about the good heart, given in Matthew 5:21–48, deal with all those day-to-day attitudes that keep the pot of human evil boiling: contempt and hostility toward others, sexual lust and disgust in the heart, the will to manipulate others verbally, revenge and payback, and so forth. These, Jesus tells us, can all be replaced with genuine compassion, purity, and goodwill as we grow new "insides."

And when we ask, "How?" he points us back to his first lesson, above, which assures us of our place and future in God's eternal purposes. In the clear light of who we are in God's eyes, our angers and lusts seem silly and repulsive, since we see them as God sees them.

Then he invites us to follow him into his practices, such as solitude, silence, study, service, worship, etc.—we call them "spiritual disciplines." There, with him, the readinesses to do evil that inhabit our bodily members through long practice are gradually removed, to an ever-increasing degree. Our "flesh" increasingly comes to the side of our spirit and God's Spirit in service to God. The disciplines for the spiritual life are a central part of the crucial "in-formation" which Jesus brings to us, and we dare not neglect it.

Then, as we are advancing in the first two areas of Jesus's teaching, he will begin to teach us in a third area of absolutely vital information. We must learn of his positive interactions and involvements with us in the concrete occasions of our day-to-day activities. When we act "in his name," we act on his behalf, and he always involves himself in the process. We have to learn how this works, and he will certainly teach us as we *expect* him to move in our circumstances and are attentive to his actions.

I have personally experienced this "interaction" in many types of contexts, from family matters to large-scale writing projects, intense committee meetings or counseling sessions, speaking occasions, or repairing a broken water pipe or automobile. You may be very sure that if your sincere intent is to glorify God and bless others in your efforts, and you are not motivated by unloving attitudes, you will see the hand of God move with you as you expectantly do your work. Your part is simply to expect it, watch for it, give thanks as you see it, and, on the basis of your experience, encourage others to do the same.

If you trust Jesus Christ as your teacher, he will teach you in all these ways. You should always put forth your very best efforts of course, and you will always find room for improvement. But you also will certainly know the astonishing reality of God's eternal kind of life flowing through you moment by moment and forever. And the effects of your efforts will, as is seen in persons and events in the Bible, be vastly greater than what could result from your abilities alone.

CHAPTER 4

Looking Like Jesus

Divine Resources for a Changed
Life Are Always Available

S OME TIME AGO I came to realize that I did not love the
people next door. They were, by any standards, dangerous
and unpleasant people—ex-bikers who made their living
selling drugs.

They had never tried to harm my family, but the constant traffic of people buying drugs, a number of whom sat in the yard
while shooting up, began to wear down my patience. As I brooded
over them one day, indulging my irritation, the Lord helped me see
that I really had no love for them at all, that after "suffering" from
them for several years I would secretly be happy if they died so
that we could just be rid of them. I realized how little I truly cared
for nearly all the people I dealt with through the day, even when
on "religious business." I had to admit that I had never earnestly
sought to be possessed by God's kind of love, to become more like
Jesus. Now it was time to seek.

But is it possible to be like Jesus? Can we actually have the character of the heavenly Father? We know God shows sincere love for everyone and is consistently kind to even the ungrateful. Jesus likewise showed himself to be merciful, freely forgave injuries, and was glad simply to give, expecting nothing back. Is it possible, as Paul told the Ephesians (5:1), "therefore be imitators of God, as beloved children."

It is possible, I now believe, to "put on the Lord Jesus Christ" (Romans 13:14). Ordinary people in common surroundings can live from the abundance of God's Kingdom, letting the spirit and the actions of Jesus be the natural outflow from their lives. The "tree" can be made good, and the fruit will then be good as a matter of course (Matthew 12:33). This new life God imparts involves both a goal and a method.

His Heart, Our Heart

As disciples (literally *students*) of Jesus, our goal is to learn to be like him. We begin by trusting him to receive us as we are. But our confidence in him leads us toward the same kind of faith he had, a faith that made it possible for him to act as he did. Jesus's faith was expressed in his gospel of heaven's rule, the good news of the "kingdom of heaven" (Matthew 4:17). *Heaven* is a deeply significant word. From Abraham (Genesis 24:7) onward, it signified to the people of Israel the *direct availability of God* to his children, as well as *his supremacy over all that affects us.* From heaven, "the eyes of the Lord are on the righteous, and his ears are open to their cry" (Psalm 34:15; also 1 Peter 3:12).

Jesus was concerned to pass on to his followers this reality of heaven's rule that undergirded his life. When he sent his twelve friends out on their first mission, he told them it was like sending "sheep in the midst of wolves" (Matthew 10:16). It would be butterflies against machine guns. Nevertheless—imagine sheep being told this!—there was no need for them to fear. Two sparrows cost a penny. Yet not one falls upon the earth "apart from your Father." Heaven is so close that even the hairs on our heads are numbered. "So do not be afraid," Jesus tells us. "You are of more value than many sparrows" (Matthew 10:29–31).

Avoiding Dreary Substitutes

Living under the governance of heaven frees and empowers us to love as God loves. But outside the safety and sufficiency of heaven's rule, we are too frightened and angry to really love others, or even ourselves, and so we arrange dreary substitutes in the form of pleasures of various kinds and "loves." A contemporary wording of Jesus's comparison of God's kind of love, agape, and what normally passes for love might be "What's so great if you love those who love you? Terrorists do that! If that's all your 'love' amounts to, God certainly is not involved. Or suppose you are friendly to 'our kind of people.' So is the Mafia!" (Matthew 5:46–47).

Now reflect: Has your heart gone out in generous blessing to someone who has insulted or humiliated you? Can you work without thought of gain for the well-being of someone who openly despises you, maybe has told you to drop dead? Are you enthusiastically pulling for the success of someone competing with you for favor, position, or financial gain? That is what those possessed and permeated by God's kind of love find themselves doing.

A much-used doormat says, "Welcome, friends!" Could yours also genuinely welcome enemies? When you lend a dress, a stereo, a car, or some tools or books, are you able to release them with no hope of seeing them again, as Luke 6:35 suggests we should? I do a good bit of my own mechanical and carpentry work, and I have a good supply of tools—which neighbors soon discover. I am glad for opportunities to lend a chain saw, an ax, a crescent wrench, or pliers, for I see them as a true spiritual exercise in abandonment to God. Still with a twinge of self-concern here and there, I am learning to love others in these little things that truly matter to human relationships.

A "Golden Triangle"

If this life of faith and love from heaven is the goal of the disciple of Jesus, the natural fulfillment of the new life in Christ, how can we enter into it? While it is in one sense a result of God's presence within us, the New Testament also describes a process involved in our "putting on" the Lord Jesus Christ. It is repeatedly discussed in the Bible under three essential aspects, each inseparable from the other, all interrelated. This process could be presented in a "golden triangle" of spiritual transformation, for it is as precious as gold to the disciple, and each of its aspects is as essential to the whole process as three sides are to a triangle.

One aspect or side of our triangle is the faithful acceptance of everyday problems. By enduring trials with patience, we can reach an assurance of the fullness of heaven's rule in our lives.

James, the Lord's brother, began his message to the church by instructing us to be "supremely happy" when troubles come upon us: "When all kinds of trials and temptations crowd into your lives, my brothers, don't resent them as intruders, but welcome them as friends! Realize that they come to test your faith and to produce in you the quality of endurance" (James 1:2–3). When endurance or patience has been given full play in the details of day-to-day existence, it will make us "perfect and complete, lacking in nothing" (1:4).

Certainly James learned this from Jesus, his older brother, during more than twenty years of sometimes rancorous family life (John 7:2–8). We must never forget that for most of his life Jesus was what we today would call a blue-collar worker, a tradesman, an "independent contractor." His hands had calluses from using the first-century versions of hammers, drills, axes, saws, and planes. He was known in his village simply as "the carpenter."

There James saw him practice all he later preached. We know what it is like to "do business with the public." So did Jesus. Every single thing that Jesus taught us to do was something he had put into daily practice in circumstances just like ours. In the trials of his everyday existence, in family and village life, he verified the sufficiency of God's care for those who simply trust him and obey him. And, at least in retrospect, James understood. Once he saw who his older brother really was, he realized the power of patience in the events of daily life—manifested above all by an inoffensive tongue (James 3:2)—as the path in which God's character is fulfilled in our lives.

Opening Our Lives to the Spirit

The second side of our triangle is interaction with God's Spirit in and around us. As Paul points out, living in the Spirit allows us to "walk in" the Spirit (Galatians 5:25). This all-powerful, creative personality, the promised "strengthener," the Paraclete of John 14, gently awaits our invitation to him to act upon us, with us, and for us.

The presence of the Holy Spirit can always be recognized by the way He moves us toward what Jesus would be and do (John 16:7–15). When we inwardly experience the heavenly sweetness and power of life—the love, joy, and peace—that Jesus knew, that is the work of the Spirit in us.

Outwardly, life in the Spirit manifests itself in two ways. *Gifts* of the Spirit will enable us to perform some specific function—such as service or healing or leading worship—with effects clearly beyond those of our own making. These gifts serve God's purposes among His people, but they do not necessarily signify the state of our heart.

The *fruit* of the Spirit, in contrast, gives a sure sign of transformed *character*. When our deepest attitudes and dispositions are those of Jesus, it is because we have learned to let the Spirit foster his life in us. Paul confessed, "I have been crucified with Christ; and it is no longer I who live, but it is Christ who lives in me" (Galatians 2:19–20). The outcome of Christ living within us through the Spirit is fruit: "love, joy, peace, patience, kindness, generosity, faithfulness, gentleness, and self-control" (Galatians 5:22–23; see also John 15:8).

Both gifts and fruit are the result, not the reality, of the Spirit's presence in our lives. What brings about our transformation into Christ-likeness is our direct, personal interaction with Christ through the Spirit. The Spirit makes Christ present to us and draws us toward his likeness. It is as we thus behold the "glory of the Lord" that we are constantly "transformed into the same image from one degree of glory to another; for this comes from the Lord, the Spirit" (2 Corinthians 3:18).

The Disciplines of Christ-likeness

The third side of our triangle is made up of spiritual disciplines. These are special activities, many engaged in by Jesus himself, such as solitude and study, service and secrecy, fasting and worship. They are ways in which we undertake to follow the New Testament mandate to put to death or "make no provision for" the merely earthly aspects of our lives and to put on the new person (Colossians 3:9–10; Ephesians 4:22–24).

The emphasis in this dimension of spiritual transformation is upon *our* efforts. True, we are given much, and without grace we can do nothing, but our action is also required. "Try your hardest," Peter directs us (2 Peter 1:5). *We* are to add virtue to our faith, knowledge to our virtue, self-control to our knowledge, patience to our self-control, godlikeness to our patience, brotherly love to our godlikeness, and agape to our brotherly love (2 Peter 1:5–7).

Paul urges us "as God's chosen ones, holy and beloved," to renew our inner selves with organs ("bowels," in the King James Version) of mercy, kindness, humbleness of mind, meekness, long-suffering, forbearance, forgiveness, and agape (Colossians 3:12–14). We should not only want to be merciful, kind, unassuming, and patient persons but also be *making plans* to become so. We are to find out, that is, what prevents and what promotes mercifulness and kindness and patience in our souls, and we are to remove hindrances to them as much as possible, carefully substituting that which assists Christ-likeness.

Many well-meaning people, to give an example, cannot succeed in being kind because they are too rushed to get things done. Haste has worry, fear, and anger as close associates; it is a deadly enemy of kindness, and hence of love. If this is our problem, we may be greatly helped by a day's retreat into solitude and silence, where we will discover that the world survives even though we are inactive. There we might prayerfully meditate to see clearly the damage done by our unkindness, and honestly compare it to what, if anything, is really gained by our hurry. We will come to understand that for the most part our hurry is really based upon pride, self-importance, fear, and lack of faith, and rarely upon the production of anything of true value for anyone.

Perhaps we will end up making plans to pray daily for the people with whom we deal regularly. Or we may resolve to ask associates for forgiveness for past injuries. Whatever comes of such prayerful reflection, we may be absolutely sure that our lives will never be the same, and that we will enjoy a far greater richness of God's reality in our lives.

In general, then, we "put on" the new person by regular activities that are in our power, and we become what we could not be by direct effort. If we take note of and follow Jesus in what he did when he was not ministering or teaching, we will find ourselves led and enabled to behave as he did when he was "on the spot."[1]

The single most obvious trait of those who profess Christ but do not grow into Christ-likeness is their refusal to take the reasonable and time-tested measures for spiritual growth. I almost never meet someone in spiritual coldness, perplexity, distress, and failure who is regular in the use of those spiritual exercises that will be obvious to anyone familiar with the contents of the New Testament.

Like Stars in a Dark World

The three sides of the "golden triangle" of spiritual transformation belong together. No one of the three will give us a heart and life like Christ's without the other two. None can take the place of any other. Yet each, connected to the others, will certainly bring us to ever-increasing Christ-likeness.

In Philippians 2, the apostle draws all three together in one grand statement: "You must work out your own salvation in fear and trembling; for it is God who works in you, inspiring both the will and the deed, for his own chosen purpose. Do all you have to do without complaint or wrangling. Show yourselves guileless and above reproach, faultless children of God in a warped and crooked generation, in which you shine like stars in a dark world" (Philippians 2:12–15).

When we accept moment-to-moment events and tribulations as the place where we receive God's provision, we patiently anticipate the action of His Spirit in our lives. In hope, we do our best to find and implement the ways in which our inner self can take on the character of the children of the Highest. This is the path of radical change—change sufficient to meet the needs of the world and prepare a people to be the habitation of God.

CHAPTER 5

The Key to the
Keys to the Kingdom

A PASTOR CONFIDED IN ME that he loved to spend a short while reading the newspaper in the morning, but felt it would be irresponsible. This was only one of many things he either denied himself or felt guilty about doing because of his perceived workload. He was burdened by the task of making a small church succeed in circumstances that were very hard. No matter how hard he tried, it would never be enough so long as his attendance was not large and growing and he did not have an appropriate building and cash flow.

In fact, however, the inner burden he carried was not much different in quantity from that of many ministers prospering in larger, more "successful" churches, and from that of many not in "full-time Christian service." The need to achieve is too great. Invariably, it is the personal and spiritual life of the minister that suffers. And—like doctors, lawyers, and other professionals today—he often comes to feel strongly that the circumstances in which he works are in conflict with the very goals for which he entered his profession in the first place. Heightened frustration and disappointment go hand in hand with decreasing strength, peace, and joy. The conditions and habits of our work in ministry often seem incompatible with the life that Jesus lived and surely offers to us.

But it does not have to be so. There is a way of getting hold of our concrete ministerial situation and finding the joy, strength, and vision in service which obviously characterized Jesus himself, as well as many of his fellow workers and friends through the ages.

The One we work for and with has placed in our hands the keys to the Kingdom of the Heavens (Matthew 16:19). Setting aside centuries of ecclesiastical controversy over the meaning of this passage, we need to simply understand that our confidence in Jesus as the one who "has say over all things in heaven and in earth" (Matthew 28:18) can develop into practical access to the riches of the Kingdom. These riches, in turn, make it possible for us to do the work we have to do, and to live our lives, in the strength, joy, and peace of Christ.

Having the keys is not a matter of controlling access to the Kingdom, as is often thought. Keys do not first mean the right to control access, but the enjoyment of access. Imagine a man who carefully kept his doors locked and his keys in hand, but never went into his house! Having access to the Kingdom, living in it, is what matters.

The meaning of Matthew 16:19 is, therefore, not fundamentally different from Matthew 6:33: "Seek more than anything else to act with the Kingdom of God and to have His kind of goodness, and all else you need will be added" (paraphrase). Or Romans 8:32: "He who did not withhold his own Son, but gave him up for all of us, will He not with Him also give us every thing else?" Or the well-known Philippians 4:19: "And my God will fully satisfy every need of yours according to his riches in glory in Christ Jesus."

But if the abundance is here, enough even to defeat the "Gates of Hell," why are we not thriving in it? The answer is that we must have and use our key to the keys. The abundance of God to our lives, our families, and our ministries is not passively received or imposed and does not happen to us by chance. It is claimed and put into action by our active, intelligent pursuit of it. We must seek out ways to live and act in union with the flow of God's Kingdom life that should come through our relationship with Jesus.

There is, of course, no question of doing this purely on our own. But we must act. Grace is opposed to earning, not to effort. And *it is well-directed, decisive, and sustained effort that is the key to the keys of the Kingdom and to the life of restful power in ministry and life that those keys open to us.*

What are some practices that will make the keys, given in response to our faith in Jesus as Messiah, effective in our lives as Christ-followers and as ministers? We strongly need to see the manifest hand of God in what we are and what we do. We need to be sure *He* is pulling the load, bearing the burden—which we are all too ready to assume is up to us alone. We must understand that He is in charge of the *outcome* of our efforts, and that the *outcome* will be good, right. And all of this is encompassed in one biblical term, "Sabbath."

The Sabbath, Jesus said, was made for humankind (Mark 2:27). That is, it serves human life in essential ways. Without it, life cannot be what it should be. That is why it is given in the Ten Commandments, at the heart of the moral law. It is not something we have to do because God has arbitrarily required it of us, a pointless hoop He would have us jump through. It is His gift to us. At the same time it makes clear that our life and our ministry are *also* His gift to us.

Sabbath is a way of life (Hebrews 4:3, 9–11). It sets us free from bondage to our own efforts. Only in this way can we come to the power and joy of a radiant life in ministry and work, a blessing to all we touch. And yet Sabbath is almost totally absent from the existence of contemporary Christians and their ministers.

What is Sabbath? Biblically, it is mainly a day, once a week, when we *do no work*. "Six days you shall labor and do all your work. But the seventh day is a Sabbath to the Lord your God; you shall not do any work" (Exodus 20:9–10). It was also a year, once every seven years, when God's covenant people did not sow seed, prune vines, or store up harvest (Leviticus 25:4–7). And to the question, "How are we going to eat in the seventh year?" God replied, "I will order My blessing for you in the sixth year, so that it will yield a crop for three years" (Leviticus 25:21).

The moral principle certainly applies as well to our non-agrarian, contemporary life, though our faith will be greatly challenged in working out the details. Very practically, Sabbath is simply "casting all your anxiety on Him," to find that in actual fact "He cares for you" (1 Peter 5:7; see also Psalm 37:3–8). It is *using* the keys to the Kingdom to receive the resources for abundant living and ministering.

Three practices or spiritual disciplines are especially helpful in making Sabbath real in the midst of our life: *solitude, silence,* and *fasting*. These are three of the central disciplines of abstinence long practiced by the followers of Jesus to help them find and keep a solid footing in the Kingdom that cannot be moved—in the midst of a busy and productive life, or even a life of trial, conflict, and frustration.

For most of us, Sabbath will not become possible without extensive, regular practice of solitude. That is, we must practice time alone, out of contact with others, in a comfortable setting outdoors or indoors, doing no work. We must not take our work with us into solitude, or it will evade us—not even in the form of Bible study, prayer, or sermon preparation, for then we will not be alone. An afternoon walking by a stream or on the beach, in the mountains, or sitting in a comfortable room or yard is a good way to start. This should become a weekly practice. Then perhaps a day, or a day and a night, in a retreat center where we can be alone. Then perhaps a weekend or a week, as wisdom dictates.

This will be pretty scary at first for most of us. But we must not try to get God to "do something" to fill up our time. That will only throw us back into work. The command is "Do no work." Just make space. Attend to what is around you. Learn that you don't have to *do* to *be*. Accept the grace of doing nothing. Stay with it until you stop jerking and squirming.

Solitude well practiced will break the power of busyness, haste, isolation, and loneliness. You will see that the world is not on your shoulders after all. You will find yourself, and God will find you in new ways. Joy and peace will begin to bubble up within you and arrive from things and events around you. Praise and prayer will come to you and from within you. With practice, the "soul anchor" established in solitude will remain solid when you return to your ordinary life with others.

Silence also brings Sabbath to you. Silence means quietness, freedom from sounds except natural ones like breathing, bird songs, and wind and water gently moving. It also means not talking. Silence completes solitude, for without it you cannot be alone. You remain subject to the pulls and pushes of a world that exhausts you and keeps you in bondage, distracting you from God and your own soul. Far from being a mere absence, silence allows the reality of God to stand in the midst of your life. It is like the wind of eternity blowing in your face. Not for nothing does the Psalmist say, "Be still and know that I am God." God does not ordinarily compete for our attention. In silence we come to attend.

When we stop talking, we *abandon ourselves* to reality and to God. We position ourselves to attend rather than to adjust things with our words. We stop our shaping and negotiating, our "spinning." How much of our energy goes into that! We let things stand. We trust God with what others shall think.

Of course there is a time to talk, as there is a time to be with others. But we are not safe and rich in talk and companionship unless our souls are strong in solitude and silence. If we have heard the good news and have come to trust our Savior, he will meet with us through extensive solitude and silence to stabilize his love, joy, and peace in us. His character will increasingly become ours—easily, thoroughly. You rarely find any person who has made great progress in the spiritual life who did not at some point have much time in solitude and silence.

A pastor who has been discovering all this writes, "As I have slowed my life down through silence and solitude, I have discovered both the wickedness hidden by a hurried life as well as the wonder and delight my Father has in me. Oddly, through intentional times of practicing spiritual disciplines, my walk with Jesus has become more spontaneous. He is present in more of my day. I have loved others better, and seen progress made in overcoming anger and the desire to have things my way. In a nutshell, Jesus has greater access to and control over my life. I'm more in tune to the still small voice of the Spirit."

Fasting is another long-proven way of finding our way into Sabbath, where we live and do our work from the hand of God. In fasting we abstain from our ordinary food to some significant degree and for some significant length of time. Like solitude and silence, it is not done to impress God or merit favor, nor because there is anything wrong with food. Rather, it is done that we may consciously experience the direct sustenance of God to our body and our whole person. We are using the keys to access the Kingdom.

This understanding of fasting is clearly indicated by Jesus in Matthew 4:4 (with its back reference to Deuteronomy 8:2–6) and in John 4:32–34. Fasting is, indeed, feasting. When we have learned well to fast, we will not suffer from it. It will bring strength and joy. We will not be miserable, and so Jesus tells us not to look miserable (Matthew 6:16). Was he suggesting that we fake a condition of joy and sufficiency when we fast? Surely not. He knew that we would "have meat to eat" that others "know not of." I and many others can report that we have repeatedly verified this in experience.

Fasting is one way of seeking and finding the actual Kingdom of God present and active in our lives. And because we are then more immersed in the reality of the Kingdom, practically utilizing the keys, our lives take on the character and power of Jesus. This will assure us that our work is his work and that he is working. Though we act, and often work hard, it is after all not our battle, and the outcome is in his hands. We don't "battle" outcomes.

Another pastor had this to say about his experience with fasting: "Surprisingly, after the fast is when I began to realize something from the fast. I came back from the fast with a clearer sense of purpose and a renewed sense of power in my ministry. The anger which I unleashed at my wife and children was less frequent and the materialism that was squeezing the life out of my spirituality had loosened its grip." Strange, perhaps, but profound!

Yet another pastor said, "It is now my regular practice to fast before and during times I preach. I have a deeper sense of dependency and of the immense power of the spoken word. This has been demonstrated by the dear individual in my congregation who runs our tape ministry. She said that since January of this year, her orders for sermon tapes have doubled. 'I can't explain it,' she said, 'but whatever it is, keep it up!'"

Experimental, prayerful implementation of solitude, silence, fasting—and other appropriate practices, such as service, fellowship, worship, and study (there is no such thing as a complete *list* of spiritual disciplines)—will certainly liberate us into the riches of Kingdom living. *They* are the key to the keys. We do not have to live under the thumb of our circumstances. For most, it is a considerable test of faith to take control of how they spend their time. But that is up to us. And putting time-tested, biblical disciplines for the spiritual life into sensible practice will soon lead us into an abundance of the life that is eternal in quality and power.

SPIRITUAL FORMATION AND THE DEVELOPMENT OF CHARACTER

CHAPTER 6

Spiritual Formation in Christ Is for the Whole Life and the Whole Person

WHEN THE LETTER OF INVITATION from Dean George and Professor McGrath came, I was happy to see that the conference was supposed to "emphasize the coinherence of theological integrity and spiritual vitality."

That is a lovely term: "coinherence." The idea it conveys is that theological integrity and spiritual vitality are to be properties of the same thing, the individual life. That's what coinherence means. When you have a lump of sugar to drop into your coffee (if you do that sort of thing), square, white, and sweet are properties that co-inhere in the same thing, the lump of sugar.

In the case of theological integrity and spiritual vitality, I think the idea is that you really can't have the one without the other. Anyone who has the one must have the other. Can we accept that meaning? If we do, then we are in real trouble with our current practices. For today the most common circumstance is that we find them, or what is claimed to be them, in separation from each other.

I will try to address some of the issues that I think are most important here, and I have eight points to cover.[1]

Jesus said, "I will show you what someone is like who comes to me, hears my words, and acts on them. That one is like a man building a house, who dug deeply and laid the foundation on rock; when a flood arose, the river burst against that house but could not shake it, because it had been well built" (Luke 6:47–48). And Jesus said, "Why do you call me 'Lord, Lord,' and do not do what I tell you?" (Luke 6:46). Again he said, "All authority is given to me in heaven and earth. Go therefore and make apprentices to me from all kinds of people, baptizing them in the name of the Father, Son and Holy Spirit" (Matthew 28:18–20). I hope you will agree with me that he didn't just mean getting them thoroughly wet as we say the words over them, but rather that "baptizing them in the name" refers to surrounding them, immersing them in the reality of the Trinitarian community. And then we are to "teach them to obey everything that I have commanded you." That would be a natural next step, completing the process Jesus assigned to his people.

Would a person be excused if he or she took these words to mean that Jesus intends *obedience* for us? The missing note in evangelical life today is not in the first instance *spirituality* but rather *obedience*. We have generated a variety of religion to which obedience is not regarded as essential.

Now, I should warn you that I'm probably going to say some things here that will irritate you, so please have mercy on me. I'm just going to go ahead and say them and count upon the Spirit of Christ to be in our midst and help us. And of course to help me as well as you. I am assured by some of my intimates that I actually have been wrong about a point or two in the past, and I accept that as a fact.

And you may think I am wrong in saying what I have just said about obedience. But I don't understand how anyone can look ingenuously at the contents of the scripture and say that Jesus intends anything else for us but obedience. So my first point is simply: life in Christ has to do with obedience to his teaching. If we don't start there, we may as well forget about any distinctively *Christian* spirituality. Such obedience is expressed in the great words as well as the small words—the great words, "Thou shalt love the Lord your God with all your heart, soul, mind, and strength, and your neighbor as yourself"; the little words, "Bless those that curse you," "Go the second mile," and so forth.

You may think you won't explicitly encounter the big words in ordinary life, and they are a bit more elusive. But you certainly will run into the small words. Even if you only do such a thing as drive an automobile in our society, you will find people who curse you, and you will be given the challenge of blessing them. And "Whoever shall give a cup of cold water to a child in my name he shall not lose his reward." And so forth. These are some of the "small" words of Christ.

Now, being alive in Christ is itself a *spiritual* matter (see John 3). So life in Christ essentially involves spirituality. I agree with our speaker of yesterday, who had some fun with the very idea of spirituality. I too have gone out on the Internet to survey the scene, and you almost want to run from what shows up when you put "spirituality" after the "www." It's unbelievable! And of course, with "Christian spirituality" one also finds there, and in life generally, a weird, weird world. But we have to remember that, all this notwithstanding, God *is s*pirit, and He is looking for those who will worship Him *in spirit* and in truth. I believe that that means people who in the core of their being, beyond all appearance in the physical world by means of their body, want to stand clear and right before God. And they are people who wholly devote their innermost being—the heart, will, or human spirit—to doing so.

God is looking for such people. And occasionally He might find someone who was not perfectly guided doctrinally or practically, but *was* looking for Him and trying to worship Him in spirit and truth. He might just communicate with such a person and enliven his or her spirit with His Spirit. He might lead that person onward toward Himself, whereas there isn't much hope for one who is not seeking to worship Him in spirit and in truth. Paul says in Philippians 3:3, "For it is we who are the circumcision, who worship in the Spirit of God and boast in Christ Jesus and have no confidence in the flesh." That means we put confidence in the spiritual: our spirit together with His Spirit (Romans 8; 2 Corinthians 4, 5).

Now, many of you will know that the "flesh" most often shows up in the scripture, not in association with "cigarettes and whiskey and wild, wild women," but with *religious* activities. When Paul in Philippians 3:3 says that he too has "reason for confidence in the flesh," he proceeds to give us a list of *religious credentials* that is quite overwhelming. When to the Corinthians Paul talks about *carnal* Christians, he is referring to people who are disputing about who is the best speaker and leader in the church. This is a sobering thought when you consider what is routinely done among us today. The flesh stands, basically, for the natural—the spiritually or divinely unassisted abilities of human beings. And it is possible in our religious activities to depend entirely upon the flesh *in this sense*.

I don't have time here to go through all of Romans 8:1–14, but I beg you to study it carefully: "There is therefore now no condemnation for those who are in Christ Jesus. For the law of the Spirit of life in Christ Jesus has set you free from the law of sin and death" (Romans 8:1–2). I say to you very soberly that this is *not* a passage about the *forgiveness of sins.* And, indeed, I should just state at this point that we have a serious problem within our usual evangelical hermeneutic of reading passages that are *not* about forgiveness of sins as if they were, when they are really about *new life* (that is, foundational spirituality) in Christ.

One of the most famous of these passages is John 3. John 3 is not a forgiveness passage. It is about "life from above." It's about spiritual life. It's about life in the Spirit and about those who are born of the Spirit. And when you come to the end of that great passage in Romans 8:1–14 you find, "All who are led by the Spirit of God are children of God." And as you study that passage you will realize, I think, that Paul is referring to a power that enters our life, a spiritual power that comes with regeneration. And this power is, of course, God Himself and all of the instrumentalities at His disposal, from the Holy Spirit Himself to the resurrected Christ in his Kingdom, to the power of the written Word, to the angelic ambassadors, to other individuals who are heirs of salvation, and to the spiritual life and treasures that are in the body of Christ, visible as well as triumphant.

What then is *spirit? Spirit is unbodily personal reality and power.* In the way you might expect or hope for—or fear—from someone who spends most of his time working in the field of philosophy, I'm going to try to use words very carefully here. One of the things I find most distressing in the current scene is that many people have no concept of *spirit* at all. As a result, God becomes, for many Christians, little more than an oblong blur. We have people today in "Christian" settings who believe in Jesus but not in God. They do not have a clear enough idea of God to form a belief about Him. And much of their problem derives from their lack of understanding of the spiritual type of being.

Biblically, it is God who is, paradigmatically, *unbodily personal power.* Everything that is bodily—the physical universe in whole and in part—comes from Him and depends upon Him. Spirit can *enter into* and *act with* body (as is also the case with the human spirit), but it is not *from* body, even in the human case. It does not derive from the physical. I wish I had time to talk in length on this point and do some of the requisite philosophical work in relation to it, but here I simply cannot.

Spirit is *personal,* not impersonal. None of that "the force be with you" stuff is relevant here. This is one of the major things we have to understand in today's context. Of course, the personal nature of spirit is seen at its highest and clearest in the Trinitarian nature of God. "God is in himself a sweet society," an old Puritan writer used to say. What personality is, is finally understandable only in the light of the Trinitarian nature of God. God is Spirit. He is personal reality and power—the power that works by thought and choice and evaluation, not a blind force that can be manipulated if you can only find the correct technique.

What you see when the veil is drawn back on the many "spiritualities" of our day is that they are so many versions of *idolatry.* They are nothing but human attempts to use human means to achieve identity and power for the individual. Idolatry is marked by the will to use God for our purposes. So many of our "spiritualities" today, including many that go under the name of "Christian," are really forms of idolatry. I could tell you one funny story after another illustrating this—not "ha-ha funny" but "weird funny." "Funny" that makes you want to weep.

I was leading a retreat at a Catholic retreat center some time ago, and one of the staff came around to make an announcement that included the line "Father So-and-So will be holding sessions on Zen spirituality at such and such a time. Father So-and-So is famous for *reintroducing* Buddhist meditation into Catholic theology." Reintroducing? Many people today in the broad fields of spirituality actually think that Zen spirituality was seen in Jesus and unfortunately lost until recently, when some have reintroduced it. Zen spirituality is one form of idolatry of the human self.

It may help us at this point to refer to the printed abstract for this talk. They kindly allowed me to put a little more into the abstract than perhaps is usual. But we really need to understand what spirituality is, and we do that by attending to spiritual *life*. You will find the words printed here:

> *Spirituality and spiritual formation are whole life matters. A "spiritual life" for the human being consists in that range of activities in which, being brought to spiritual birth by God's initiative through the Word, he or she cooperatively interacts with God and with the spiritual order ("kingdom") deriving from God's personality and action. The result is a new overall quality of human existence with corresponding new powers. A person is a "spiritual person" to the degree that his or her life is effectively integrated into and dominated by God's Kingdom or rule. For the "babe in Christ," much of their embodied and concretely socialized personality is not under the direction of God, and the reintegration of their whole life under God is not yet achieved.*

It is very important for us to hold on to this language, because spirituality as now generally understood usually refers to a *human dimension,* not to the power of God. Sometimes it even refers to the power of demons and to the power of the devil, because he too is a spiritual being, in the sense explained above.

In contrast, a spirituality, as that term has now come to be used, simply refers to a *way of conducting religious life.*[2] A spirituality may then be no more than an exercise of human abilities. So now we have Quaker spirituality, Franciscan spirituality, Benedictine spirituality, and even Baptist spirituality. These may or may not consist of activities and forms of living that one could engage in if there were no God at all.

It is of course true that there are different ways of "doing" religion. There is a way Catholics do it, Baptists do it, Hindus do it, and so forth. And these mark their practitioners in easily discernible ways. A few years ago I got on the plane in Chicago to go to Louisville, and everyone on that plane looked like a Baptist to me. There is an outward form of being Baptist. Now, I can't actually state how Baptists look—I can't say what it is. But I often can recognize it because I've been in the middle of it all my life.

That is why I find a special thrill in standing here under the picture of Lottie Moon, up there in the dome. She has been a part of my life since I was a child: the yearly missions offering, teaching about Lottie Moon's life, and so on. I'm so glad to see her standing up there by all these men. She's great. It's a thrill to be a part of what she's part of. All of this relates to the fact that, as Paul says to the Corinthians, "we have this treasure in earthen vessels" (2 Corinthians 4:7). You cannot avoid having a vessel. You have a Baptist vessel, and you have a Benedictine vessel, and a Quaker vessel, and so forth.

The problem comes when we mistake the vessel for the treasure, for *the treasure is the life and power of Jesus Christ.* We have to have a form of life, a vessel, a "spirituality," if you wish. None of us are given to be entirely spiritual beings now. Being bodily and therefore social is a part of us. I will eternally be the son of my parents. I will always be the son of Albert and Mamie Willard. And I will always be the person who was brought up in the First Baptist Church of Buffalo, Missouri, and the First Baptist Church of Willow Springs, Missouri, and Shiloh Baptist Church in Rover, Missouri. I thank God for all that. But to make that spirituality my life—that's the point at which I may begin to think that being a good Baptist is more important than being a good Christian, than being obedient with my whole person to Jesus Christ. At that point I am back in flesh and have become spiritually off balance.

Now, substitute for "Baptist" anything you want. It doesn't make much difference. It is all the same if a spirituality is just a way of conducting religious life. The problem is that conducting the religious life can become an entirely cultural kind of thing. And we can idolize our religious culture. There are many, many ways of doing this. It is so important for us to remember that *a culture can capture us and shut off our access to the supernatural spirituality of the Kingdom of God,* as explained in John 3 and Romans 8, for example.

I'm sorry to say this, but too much of what we call Christian is *not* a manifestation of the supernatural life of God in our souls. Too much of what we call Christian is really just human. And now I'm going to say something really terrible, so brace yourselves or stop your ears. The church of Jesus Christ is not necessarily present when there is a correct administration of the sacrament and faithful preaching of the Word of God. The church of God is present where people gather together in the power of the resurrected life of Jesus Christ. It is possible to have the administration of the sacraments and the preaching of the Word of God and to have it be simply a human exercise. And the misunderstanding of the church in this respect is one of the things that create a primary problem for the integration of theology and spirituality. Because, as was emphasized yesterday, a bad theology will kill any prospects of a spirituality that comes from life in Christ.

Now where have we got? The first of my eight points was that life in Christ, and therefore *biblical* spirituality, has to do with obedience to Christ. My second point was that life in Christ is a matter of the "spirit." My third point was that spiritual life is a matter of living our lives *from* the reality of God. My fourth point is that Christian spirituality is supernatural *because* obedience to Christ is supernatural and cannot be accomplished except in the power of a "life from above."

The will to obey is the engine that pulls the train of spirituality in Christ. But spirituality in many Christian circles has simply become another dimension of Christian consumerism. We have generated a body of people who consume Christian services and think that that is Christian faith. Consumption of Christian services replaces obedience to Christ. And spirituality is one more thing to consume. I go to many, many conferences and talk about these things, and so often I see these people who are just consuming more Christian services.

But we *must* talk about spirituality, and this naturally leads us to talk also about *spiritual disciplines.* Spiritual disciplines are activities in our power that we engage in to enable us to do what we cannot do by direct effort. The singing of hymns, for example, is a major spiritual discipline. I refer not just to singing them in church, but to singing them throughout our daily life. We need to say, under this fourth point—that Christian spirituality is supernatural and focused on obedience to Christ—that when we come to sing our hymns, we must keep our mind and will alive to what we are singing. Only so will the outcome be supernatural.

I love that old hymn we sang last night, "Draw me nearer, nearer, nearer, precious Lord, to the cross where thou hast died." But what does that mean to be drawn nearer to the cross of Jesus? What does that mean in practice? Does that just mean a warmer heart now and then, or does it mean *living* in step with the Jesus of the cross and resurrection? I think it means the latter. I think it means union in action. *Union in action with the triune God is Christian spirituality.* That is where the life is drawing its substance from God. Draw me nearer! Or, "Grow in grace." What does that mean?

It doesn't mean get more forgiveness. I will return to that point in a moment.

My fifth point concerns *spiritual formation*. "Spiritual formation" refers to the *process* of shaping our spirit and giving it a definite character. It means the formation of our spirit in conformity with the Spirit of Christ. Of course it involves the Holy Spirit in action. But the focus of spiritual formation is the formation of *our* spirit. (Forgive me if I am wrong here, but I equate spirit, will, and heart in the human being. They are the same component of the human being, referred to in different ways.) And if you could look back to the abstract in your little booklet again, you will see the wording "Spiritual formation in Christ is the *process* whereby the inmost being of the individual (the heart, will, or spirit) takes on the quality or character of Jesus himself." That's what spiritual formation is, and we need to say something about why there's been such a buzz around this terminology in recent years.

Spiritual formation is, of course, not a new topic within the church at large, but it is a new topic in evangelical circles. I think the reason is that we have come into a time of obvious need for something new and deeper. "Discipleship" is a term that has pretty well lost its meaning because of the way it has been misused. Discipleship on the theological right has come to mean preparation for soul winning, under the direction of parachurch efforts that had discipleship farmed out to them because the local church really wasn't doing it. On the left, discipleship has come to mean some form of social activity or social service, from serving soup lines to political protest to . . . whatever. The term "discipleship" has currently been ruined so far as any solid psychological and biblical content is concerned.

Another thing that has led to the interest in spiritual formation is the breakdown of the significance of denominational differences. It is rare that you find anyone today who thinks that their denominational identity ensures very much in the way of Christian substance. Some might still believe it does, but those will be pretty narrow circles. Sociologically we have lost the significance of denominational membership. Most people who are confessing Christians, evangelicals or not, drift from one kind of church to another today and simply look to the local congregation and its leadership as a basis of choosing their church, not to denomination—or certainly not to it alone. Most younger people, especially, have no idea of what the differences of denomination amount to. Recently the daughter of an acquaintance asked him, "Which chain do we belong to?"

I would be quite interested to know, for example, how many Baptist churches now, as they did in my youth, insist, when you take membership in them, that you move your membership to another *Baptist* church when you move to another location. I hope I will get some data on this, because I would really like to know about it.

With the breakdown of the denominational language and association, in any case, there is a need for a new language, and spiritual formation has stepped into that void to express the essence and depth of our commitment to Christ. It is, indeed, an interdenominational or nondenominational language. But the main thing that it tries to do is refer us to the need for *inward* transformation, and it is now statistically and anecdotally common to find that Christians generally do not differ significantly from non-Christians in our culture. Some Christians do. If you survey correctly, you will find that there is a group of Christians who do differ radically from non-Christians, but that kind of commitment is, even among Christians themselves, understood to be a kind of spiritual option or luxury. So my fifth point is this: spiritual formation is the process whereby the inmost being of the individual takes on the quality or character of Jesus himself.

My sixth point is that such a process is not a matter of the human spirit or heart *only*. We must be careful about how we talk about the person and its several parts. Rather, spiritual formation is a whole life process dealing with change in every essential part of the person. We don't work on just our spirit, but on everything that makes up our personality.

Spiritual formation does not aim at controlling action. This is an absolutely crucial point, and one that distinguishes spiritual formation in Christ from what, primarily, is aimed at in most twelve-step groups. (Not to diminish the good such groups accomplish!) If in spiritual formation you focus on action alone, you will fall into the deadliest of legalisms and you will kill other souls and die yourself. You will get a social conformity. That has happened over and over again in the past, and it is where the various "spiritualities" past and present begin to exact a dreadful price—focusing on the outward activities and the actions, not on the inward person, not on the "spirit." God is looking for those who worship him in truth and in spirit. We cannot fake before God. We should remember that God looks on the heart, man looks on the outward appearance. To focus on action alone is to fall into pharisaism of the worst kind and to kill the soul.

So spiritual formation is a holistic process, and now to help us grasp this point I am going to suggest that you create your own visual aid. If you would draw a circle about the size of a half-dollar on a piece of paper and write in it the words "spirit," "heart," and "will." And then around that draw another circle and label it "mind," including thought and feeling. The third circle is "body." The fourth circle is "social relations." Your final circle is your soul. So you have spirit (will), mind (thoughts and feelings), body, social relations, and soul.[3]

Now, we could get in a long fight about the essential elements of the human being, but I beg off, because I need simply to make a point. If you want to divide the whole person up in other ways, be my guest. I do think that this little diagram is an adequate presentation of the self for making the point I need to make. And that is that *spiritual formation is a matter of reworking all aspects of the self.* This explains why genuine formation in Christ never leads to *privatization* or to *legalism.* Spiritual formation is not a matter of just the spirit or heart, nor even of the soul, nor of outward behavior. The spirit, heart, or will is the executive center of the self. It is where action *ultimately* comes from, and it is absolutely fundamental. But it does not operate in isolation from the mind, from the body, from the social relationships, and from the soul, nor they from it. It operates in dependence on them. So, now, if we are going to do spiritual formation, we have to work on *all* of those aspects of the human being.

And one of the greatest temptations that we face as evangelicals—for the moment I include in that what is sometimes called the charismatic stream of the church—is the idea that the personality and the heart are going to be transformed by some sort of lightning strike of the Spirit. You can call it revival or whatever you want. There is going to be this great *boom,* and then suddenly you will be transformed in every aspect of your being. There will be no need for a process—it will all be accomplished passively and immediately.

But now consider: when the people of Israel came into the Promised Land, the first city they approached was Jericho, and the walls of Jericho, we know, *fell down* flat. Tell me, how many more walls of cities fell down flat in the conquest of the Promised Land? What did the Israelites have to do with the rest of those cities? They had to *take* them, didn't they? And we are today lulled into a false passivity by our basic teachings about the nature of salvation and the work of God in our souls. We like to quote verses like, "Without Me you can do nothing," which is absolutely true.

But we forget that *if you do nothing, it will be without Me.* And this, while not a scripture verse, is absolutely true and borne out by scripture teaching as a whole.

We today are very uneasy about human activity, and we have words like "synergism," which in some theological circles is a dirty word. But when we go that route, we will be at a loss before the call of discipleship—or the call, in Paul's language, "to put off the old person and put on the new." What we must understand is that spiritual formation is a process that involves the transformation of the whole person, and that the whole person must be *active with Christ* in the work of spiritual formation. Spiritual transformation into Christ-likeness is not going to happen to us unless we act. I'll return to that in just a moment as I conclude with my eighth point, which tries to deal with a few troublesome issues.

My seventh point will consist in illustrating how the transformation of these various aspects of the human self affects our powers at large. Think a moment about thought. Thought is a subdimension of the mind. Now, if we are going to be spiritually transformed we have to have transformation of our thought life. Remember that Paul said in Romans 1, "They refuse to retain God in their knowledge" (verse 21). Frankly, what that means is that they could not stand to think about God and about who He is. If *you* are on the throne of your life, you won't want to think about God because He is, after all, *God,* and there will not be room for both Him and anybody else on the throne of your life. And when human beings put God out of their knowledge, as Paul said, He then gives them up to themselves—a dreadful fate.

God is not pushy—for now, in any case. He is not going to overwhelm you if you don't want Him. He gives you the power to put Him out of your mind. And even if you want Him, you have to seek Him. Now, I realize that there is a sense in which He is already seeking you, and I am not trying to dispose of that, but we misunderstand what is our part and what is God's part. God is ready to act. He is acting. We are not waiting on Him; and if it doesn't hurt your theology too badly, He is waiting on us to respond. And you know we have a problem here. As I often point out to folks, today we are not only saved by grace, we are *paralyzed* by it. We will preach to you for an hour that you can do nothing to be saved, and then sing to you for forty-five minutes trying to get you to do something to be saved. That is confusing, to say the least. We really have a problem with activity and passivity in our theology. I can't begin to deal with all of that here, but I simply am calling attention to it.

We have to think about *working with* God on the contents of our minds. David says in Psalm 16:8, "I keep the Lord always before me." I keep the Lord *always* before me. *I* keep the Lord always before me. What do we say to David? Synergism! Works! "I keep the Lord always before me; because He is at my right hand, I shall not be moved." Here is *our* action at the heart of that great messianic Psalm, which I wish I had time to talk more about because it has so much to say about spiritual formation.

How, then, shall we set the Lord always before us? *Bible memorization* is absolutely fundamental to spiritual formation. If I had to—and of course I don't have to—choose between all the disciplines of the spiritual life and take only one, I would choose Bible memorization. I would not be a pastor of a church that did not have a program of Bible memorization in it, because Bible memorization is a fundamental way of filling our minds with what they need. "This book of the law shall not depart out of your mouth" (Joshua 1:8). That's where we need it! In our mouth. Now, how did it get in your mouth? Memorization. I often point out to people how much trouble they would have stayed out of if they had been muttering scripture. Our friend Bill Clinton would have done much better with that. Muttering scripture. You meditate in it day and night. What does that mean? Keep it, and therefore God, before your mind all the time. Can anyone really imagine that they have anything better to keep before their mind? No! "That you may observe to do all that is written therein, and then you will make your way prosperous, and you will have your success" (Deuteronomy 28:1–2).

I often tell people I can give them one verse that is worth more than any college education, and it is Joshua 1:8. It will guarantee them the life that they only dimly dream to be possible. How does it work? Well, I often use phrases from the Twenty-third Psalm, for example. On a given day I may renew constantly in my mind the words, "You lead me in paths of righteousness for Your name's sake." Or on a particularly difficult day I may use, "You prepare a table before me in the presence of my enemies." That's just one illustration of how to set the Lord constantly before you.

Much more could be said about the effects of transforming the arena of our thought life. But turning for a moment to the area of feeling in our personality: many people live their lives filled with anxiety or anger or contempt. They fill their lives with resentment. They willingly fill their lives with lusting. Our culture constantly excites to lust. Not just for sex, but of course sex remains one of the most powerful strings to pull to get attention and action, and we constantly have solicitation going on in this arena.

But you have to change all that in spiritual formation. After all, it is not the law of gravity. You have to change your feelings. (Of course with God's help.) If Joseph had filled his mind with thoughts of romance or sexual indulgence with Mrs. Potiphar, she would have got *him* and not just his coat (Genesis 39:7–12).

When you hear stories about men and women who have, as we say, fallen, I hope you will realize that the sad thing is not just that they fell, but what has been in their mind all along—possibly for many years or even all their life. That's where the work must be done for spiritual formation. It isn't just action control. That is the error of the Pharisee.

Think for a moment of spiritual formation in the arena of social relationships. So very much could be said here. But just think of one thing only: think of those persons who have, by the grace of God, cultivated in their relationships to others *the life of the servant.* Everywhere they are and in all that they do, they live as a servant.

You will remember that Jesus said, "I am among you as one who serves" (Luke 22:27). And he also said, "Whoever wishes to become great among you must be your servant" (Mark 10:44). By the way, it is dreadful to see this recommended as only another *technique* for succeeding in leadership. Jesus wasn't giving techniques for successful leadership. He was telling us *who the great person is.* He or she is the one who is servant of all. Being a servant shifts one's relationship to everyone. What do you think it would do to sexual temptation if you thought of yourself as a servant? What do you think it would do to covetousness? What do you think it would do to the feeling of resentment because you didn't get what you thought you deserved? I'll tell you. It will lift the burden.

These are just a few quick illustrations of how the overall transformation of the self comes about in the process of spiritual formation. I wish I had time to talk about the soul and body too, for they each have their own central role in spiritual formation. They also aim at transforming the self, the whole person. But I must now conclude. My seventh point, in case you missed it, was that the aim of spiritual formation is the transformation of the self, and that it works through transformation of thought, transformation of feeling, transformation of social relations, transformation of the body, and transformation of the soul. When we work with *all* these, transformation of the spirit (heart, will) very largely, though not entirely, takes care of itself.

Perhaps I could now just ask how much of our personal efforts, as well as our ministerial and teaching efforts, are directed toward spiritual transformation in this holistic sense. To drive the point home I often put this challenge: I do not know of a denomination or local church in existence that has as its goal to teach its people to do everything Jesus said. I'm not talking about a whim or a wish, but a *plan*.[4] I ask you sincerely, is this on *your* agenda? To teach disciples surrounded in the triune reality to do everything Jesus said? If that is your goal, you will certainly find a way to bring theological integrity and spiritual vitality together. But as you do so, you will find both your theology and your spirituality refreshingly and strongly modified.

My eighth and final point is just about some issues that always come up. And first, *grace and works*. Isn't "spiritual formation" really just another term for "works"? Yes, we're talking about if you mean, "Am I going to have to do something?" You cannot be a pew potato and simultaneously engage in spiritual formation in Christ's likeness. You have to take your whole life into discipleship to Jesus Christ, if that's what you mean by works. But on the other hand, nothing works like genuine faith or trust in God.

Much of our problem is *not*, as is often said, that we have failed to get what is in our head down in our heart. Much of what hinders us is that we have had a lot of mistaken theology in our head and it *has* gotten down into our heart. And it is controlling our inner dynamics so that the head and heart cannot, even with the aid of the Word and the Spirit, pull one another straight.

May I just give you this word? Grace is not opposed to effort, it is opposed to earning. Earning is an attitude. Effort is an action. Grace, you know, does not just have to do with forgiveness of sins alone. Many people *don't* know this, and that is one major result of the cutting down of the gospel to a theory of justification, which has happened in our time. I have heard leading evangelical spokespeople say that grace has only to do with guilt. Many people today understand justification as the only essential result of the gospel, and the gospel they preach is—and you will hear this said over and over by the leading presenters of evangelical faith—that your sins can be forgiven. That's it!

In contrast, I make bold to say, the gospel of the entire New Testament is that you can have new life now in the Kingdom of God if you will trust Jesus Christ. Not just something he did, or something he said, but trust the whole person of Christ in everything he touches—which is everything. "There is one God; there is also one mediator between God and humankind, Christ Jesus, himself human" (1 Timothy 2:5). If you would really like to be into consuming grace, just lead a holy life. The true saint burns grace like a 747 burns fuel on takeoff. Become the kind of person who routinely does what Jesus did and said. You will consume much more grace by leading a holy life than you will by sinning, because every holy act you do will have to be upheld by the grace of God. And that upholding is totally the unmerited favor of God in action. It is the life of regeneration and resurrection—*and* justification, which is absolutely vital, for our sins have to be forgiven. But justification is not something *separable* from regeneration. And regeneration naturally moves into sanctification and glorification.

If you preach a gospel that has only to do with the forgiveness of sins, on the other hand, you will be as we are today: stuck in a position where you have faith over here and obedience and abundance over there, and no way to get from here to there because the necessary bridge is discipleship. If there is anything we should know by now, it is that *a gospel of justification alone does not generate disciples.* Discipleship is a life of learning from Jesus Christ how to live in the Kingdom of God now, as he himself did. If you want to be a person of grace, then, live a holy life of discipleship, because the only way you can do that is on a steady diet of grace. Works of the Kingdom live from grace.

The second issue is *perfectionism*. People quickly become worried about this when you get really serious about spiritual formation, and with some good reason no doubt. But most of us would not have to worry about perfection for a few months at least. Still, I know many people in evangelical circles who are more stirred up over perfectionism than they are about people continuing in sin. Now, just for the record, as far as I know, we are all going to have room for improvement as long as we live.

I love this quote from St. Augustine:

> *If anyone supposes that with man, living, as he still does in this mortal life, it may be possible for him to dispel and clear off every obscurity induced by corporeal and carnal fancies, and to obtain to the serenest light of immutable truth, and to cleave constantly and unswervingly to this with a mind wholly estranged from the course of this present life, that man understands neither what he asks nor who he is that is putting such a supposition. . . . If ever the soul is helped to reach beyond the cloud by which all of the earth is covered (cf. Ecclus. XXIV, 6), that is to say, beyond this carnal darkness with which the whole terrestrial life is covered, it is simply as if he were touched with a swift coruscation, only to sink back into his natural infirmity, the desire surviving by which he may again be raised to the heights, but his purity being insufficient to establish him there. The more, however, anyone can do this, the greater is he, while the less he can do so the less is he.*[5]

No matter how far we progress, there will always be in us a subdued, glowing coal of possibility that, if blown by the right wind, will burst into a flame of iniquity. But that doesn't have to happen. As for people who plead for continuing in sin, I must ask them, "Are you planning on it?" Sometimes it sounds like they are. So my third issue is this: *we cannot have a gospel dealing only with sin.* We have to have a gospel that leads us to new life in Christ, and then spirituality can be presented as a natural development of such new life. But if we divide between justification and regeneration in such a way that the gospel is *only* "Believe Jesus died for your sins and you will go to heaven when you die," we are stuck with a theology that is inherently resistant to a vital spirituality. Now, please don't misunderstand me: that statement is strictly true, but we have come to accept "Believe Jesus died for your sins" in a way that does not involve "Believe Jesus in everything." The gospel is new life through faith in Jesus Christ. If you don't preach that, then there will be no possibility of a spirituality that is theologically sound or a theology that is spiritually vital.

The fourth and final issue under my eighth point is *the inescapability of serious process over time.* We cannot continue to hope that lightning is going to strike us and out of this we will come glowing with spirituality. I want to read just a few words that are so typical; this is actually from a charismatic writer. I don't like that language, for I don't really think there is such a thing as a noncharismatic Christian—but that's a different story. Here is what the man says in the course of bemoaning the state of the charismatic movement. He says, "The charismatic movement today is far from bad, but it is as equally as far from well." And if I may say so, that is true of the evangelical movement generally. He continues on to ask, "What must be done? I believe the answer begins with fresh spiritual fire. The fire that consumes the juvenile need for human recognition. The fire that burns without the invitation of American culture. A fire that engulfs carnality. Let the flames rise until we recall that Jesus Christ is the most dynamic force we will ever release on a decadent society. Fire-born prayer, arm us with weapons."

Now, pardon me, but I believe it is the essence of futility to talk this way. And you can translate these words out of the charismatic movement and into the evangelical. Generally expressed, baptism in the Spirit, spiritual experiences, high acts of worship, and other experiences of worship *do not transform character.* They just don't do it. I am one who has had glorious experiences, and who owes much to them. They have a special role in the spiritual life. I don't talk about the experiences I have had because I think they are between me and the Lord, and, in any case, they are to be known by their effects. They have meant a lot to me, but *they* have not transformed my character.

You or others must be the judges of how far my transformed character goes—if that is of any interest at all—but from my point of view, I can tell you that the transformation of character comes through learning how to act in concert with Jesus Christ. *Character is formed through action, and it is transformed through action,* including carefully planned and grace-sustained disciplines. To enter the path of obedience to Jesus Christ—intending to obey him and intending to learn whatever I have to learn in order to obey him—is the true path of spiritual formation or transformation.

We should expect to have lots of profound, key moments. I don't want to miss a one of them. I love them, and sometimes when I get to the end of the Lord's Prayer, having had a wonderful session in it—you can spend hours in it and submerge yourself in it—when I get to the end, I don't want to say, "Amen"—I want to say, "Whoopee! Thanks be to God! Thine is the Kingdom! Thine is the power! Thine is the glory! Forever!" "Amen" is just a little too mild.

I hope your life is full of "Whoopee!" moments. We should all have them, but they will not transform us. What transforms us is the will to obey Jesus Christ from a life that is one with his resurrected reality day by day, learning obedience through inward transformation.

Paul well understood this. We close with his words to the Colossians (3:1–4): "So if you have been raised with Christ, seek the things that are above, where Christ is, seated at the right hand of God. Set your minds on things that are above, not on things that are on earth, for you have died, and your life is hidden with Christ in God. When Christ who is your life is revealed, then you also will be revealed with him in glory."

What's the next move? Does anyone know? It is

Put to death, therefore, whatever in you is earthly: fornication, impurity, passion, evil desire, and greed (which is idolatry). On account of these the wrath of God is coming on those who are disobedient. These are the ways you also once followed, when you were living that life. But now you must get rid of all such things—anger, wrath, malice, slander, and abusive language from your mouth. Do not lie to one another, seeing that you have stripped off the old self with its practices and have clothed yourselves with the new self, which is being renewed in knowledge according to the image of its creator. (Colossians 3:5–10)

What an incredible, sweeping change of mind is this,

in which there is no longer Greek and Jew, circumcised and uncircumcised, barbarian, Scythian [the Scythian was the utter bottom of the human barrel in Paul's world], slave and free; but Christ is all and in all! As God's chosen ones, holy and beloved, clothe yourselves with compassion, kindness, humility, meekness, and patience. . . . Above all, clothe yourselves with love, which binds everything together in perfect harmony. And let the peace of Christ rule in your hearts, to which indeed you were called in the one body. And be thankful. Let the word of Christ dwell in you richly; teach and admonish one another in all wisdom; and with gratitude in your hearts sing psalms, hymns, and spiritual songs to God. (Colossians 3:11–16)

And then comes that great seventeenth verse—which solidly drives home the point of our talk, the whole-life nature of our spiritual formation in Christ: "Whatsoever you do, in word or deed, do everything in the name of the Lord Jesus, giving thanks to God the Father through him."

CHAPTER 7

Spiritual Formation in Christ

A Perspective on What It Is and How It Might Be Done

". . . until Christ is formed in you."

—Galatians 4:19

S PIRITUAL FORMATION" is a phrase that has recently rocketed onto the lips and into the ears of Protestant Christians with an abruptness that is bound to make a thoughtful person uneasy. If it is really so important, not to mention essential, then why is it so recent? It must be just another passing fad in Protestant religiosity, increasingly self-conscious and threatened about "not meeting the needs of the people." And, really, isn't spiritual formation just a little too "Catholic" for Protestants to be comfortable with?

We could forget the phrase "spiritual formation," but the fact and need would still be there to be dealt with. The spiritual side of the human being, Christian and non-Christian alike, *develops* into the reality that it becomes, for good or ill. Everyone receives spiritual formation, just as everyone gets an education. The only question is whether it is a good one or a bad one. We need to take a conscious, intentional hand in the developmental process. We need to understand what the formation of the human spirit is, and how it can best be done as Christ would have it done. This is an indispensable aspect of developing a psychology that is adequate to human life.

The reason for the recent abrupt emergence of the spiritual formation terminology into religious life is, I believe, a growing suspicion or realization that we have not done well with the reality and the need. We have counted on preaching, teaching, and knowledge or information to form faith in the hearer and have counted on faith to form the inner life and outward behavior of the Christian. But, for whatever reason, this strategy has not turned out well. The result is that we have multitudes of professing Christians who well may be ready to die but obviously are not ready to live, and can hardly get along with themselves, much less with others.

Most statistical measures and anecdotal portraits of evangelical Christians, not to mention Christians in general, show a remarkable similarity in the life-texture of Christians and non-Christians. Even among clergy, simple rest in and obedience to Christ is not something to assume without special indications; thus, we should look carefully at the whole issue of spiritual formation, especially to identify the essence of the gospel and the eternal kind of life that may correspond to it.

Too often spiritual formation is regarded as a catchall category that conveys little specific information. Gerald G. May writes, "Spiritual formation is a rather general term referring to all attempts, means, instructions, and disciplines intended towards deepening of faith and furtherance of spiritual growth. It includes educational endeavors as well as the more intimate and in-depth process of spiritual direction."[1]

It is useful, therefore, to speak of spiritual formation by distinguishing three different meanings or moments. First, identifying certain activities as spiritual work or exercise, one can think of *spiritual formation as training in these special spiritual activities*. Certainly, this is a large part of what is found in many cases to be meant by "priestly formation," or the spiritual formation of the priest, as spoken of in Catholic literature, with the recognition that such formation goes beyond overt behavior and deeply into the inner or spiritual life of the individual. Marcial Maciel's *Integral Formation of Catholic Priests* is an excellent treatment of spiritual formation as it bears upon the vocation of the priest.[2]

The Protestant counterpart is the outward behavior of the successful minister, pastor, leader, or full-time Christian worker. Spiritual formation can be thought of as the training that makes individuals successful in the aforementioned roles. Although it is recognized that the heart must be right, if one is successful enough in certain outward terms, very likely no further inquiry will be made. And, if something is known to be lacking on the inside or in the private life of the worker, as is often the case among those on a Christian staff, it may well be overlooked or justified "for the sake of the ministry."

Occasionally today one also finds those who think of spiritual formation in terms of practicing spiritual disciplines. This is a relatively recent development among evangelicals. The disciplines are regarded as part of the process of spiritual formation—which is not an altogether bad idea—or as the practice of spirituality, and formation is regarded as whatever it takes to bring us to where we are able to engage rightly in a life of spiritual disciplines. In any case, one way of thinking about spiritual formation is to identify it by references to certain specifically religious practices. Often such practices are spoken of today as a "spirituality."

Second, spiritual formation may be thought of as the *shaping of the inner life, the spirit, or the spiritual side of the human being.* The formation of the heart or will (which I believe is best taken as the spirit) of the individual, along with the emotions and intellect, is therefore the primary focus, regardless of what overt practices may or may not be involved. Here, what is formed is explicitly the spiritual dimension of the self. We speak of *spiritual* formation in this case precisely because that which is formed (the subject matter shaped) is the spiritual aspect of personality. Of course, it is assumed that there will be effects in the realm of overt practice.

Third, spiritual formation may be thought of as a *shaping by the spirit or by the spiritual realm, and by the Holy Spirit and other spiritual agencies* involved in the Kingdom of God, especially the Word of God. We speak of spiritual formation here because the *means* (or agency) that does the shaping of the human personality and life is spiritual.

Now, we need to recognize that spiritual formation in all of these senses is not necessarily a *Christian* spiritual formation. Spiritualities abound on all sides, and we are fast coming to the point where we have a spirituality of practically everything. A recent television commercial for a certain kind of truck starts out with a man saying that a truck is "a spiritual kind of thing," and he goes on to talk about the special meaning it gives to life.

I believe that spirituality is the arena in which specifically Christian faith and practice will have to struggle desperately in the coming years to retain integrity. All other "spiritualities" present themselves as equal under such slogans as "interfaith" and "ecumenism," terms that increasingly apply to all religious cultures, not just to the various branches of Christianity.

The twelve-step programs, often the bearers of great good from the viewpoint of obvious human need, are currently doing much to place anti-Christian, or at least a-Christian, spiritualities solidly in the midst of Christian congregations and lives. Also, the push for inclusivism presupposes that all cultures are equal, and how can that be unless the corresponding religions are too? Moreover, if lifestyles are equal, must they not be equal *morally?* And how can you fault whatever religion is practiced in them if they are morally equal?

How, then, are we to think about spiritual formation in a way that is faithful to the gospel and to the nature of that eternal life that is present in Christ and given to us with him?

Let us begin with practices, overt behavior. Spiritual formation *in Christ* is oriented toward explicit obedience to Christ. The language of the Great Commission, in Matthew 28, makes it clear that our aim, our job description as Christ's people, is to bring *disciples* to the point of obedience to "all things whatsoever that I have commanded you" (Matthew 28:20). Of course, this assumes that we ourselves are in obedience, having learned *how* to obey Christ. Though the inner dynamics are those of love for Christ, he left no doubt that the result would be the keeping of his commandments. "They who have my commandments and keep them are those who love me; and those who love me will be loved by my Father, and I will love them and reveal myself to them" (John 14:21).

Much of the current distress on the part of Western Christianity over how to conduct our calling as the people of Christ derives from the fact that the goal and measure of Christian spiritual formation, as described previously, is not accepted and implemented. This has long been the case, of course, reaching back for centuries. But it may be that the modern world's challenge to the church has not been equaled since its birth.

In the face of this challenge, I know of no current denomination or local congregation that has a concrete plan and practice for teaching people to do "all things whatsoever I have commanded you." Very few even regard this as something we should actually try to do, and many think it to be simply impossible. Little wonder, then, that it is hard to identify a specifically Christian version of spiritual formation among Christians and their institutions. As we depart from the mark set by the Great Commission, we increasingly find it harder to differentiate ourselves *in life* from those who are non- or even anti-Christians.

Now, of course, spiritual formation in this sense cannot be done by focusing just on actions or practices. That way leads to legalism, failure, and death, as Jesus made very clear in his "Sermon on the Mount" (Matthew 5:20). But this does not mean we must surrender the behavioral aim set up by Christ himself. We teach people to do "all things whatsoever" by shaping their hearts to love Christ and his commandments, and by training their entire personality (soul, mind, body, and to some degree even environment) to side with their new heart or spirit, which is the creative element of the self that we also call the will. To *will* (*thelein;* Romans 7:18) is not just important, it is unavoidable. But the *person* acts, and more is involved in action than willing.

Indeed, the spirit or heart may even be eager (Matthew 26:41), but unless the flesh or embodied personality as a whole is trained to go with it and support it, the follow-through in action will not occur, or will not reliably happen, or may even be in direct conflict with the spirit or will: "I do the very thing I hate!" (Romans 7:15). While the spirit or heart is the ultimate source of life (Proverbs 4:23), we do not *live* there. We live in our body and its world. Christian spiritual formation works *from* the spirit or will and from its new life "from above." But its work is not done until we have put off the old person and put on the new (Ephesians 4; Colossians 3).

This is an active, not passive, process, one that requires our clear-headed and relentless participation. It will not be done for us; however, we cannot obey Christ, or even trust him, by direct effort. What, then, are the indirect means that allow us to cooperate in reshaping the personality—the feelings, ideas, mental processes and images, and the deep readinesses of soul and body—so that our whole being is poised to go with the movements of the regenerate heart that is in us by the impact of the gospel Word under the direction and energizing of the Holy Spirit?

These means are, primarily, the disciplines for life in the Spirit: solitude and silence, prayer and fasting, worship and study, fellowship and confession, and the like. These disciplines are not, in themselves, meritorious or even required except as specifically needed. They do, however, allow the spirit or will—an infinitesimally tiny power, in itself, that we cannot count on to carry our intentions into settled, effectual righteousness—to direct the body into contexts of experience in which the whole self is inwardly restructured to follow the eager spirit into ever-fuller obedience. This is the second meaning or moment in Christian spiritual formation.

The processes of spiritual formation thus understood require precise, testable, thorough knowledge of the human self. Psychological and theological understanding of the spiritual life must go hand in hand. Neither of them is complete without the other. A psychology that is Christian, in the sense of a comprehensive understanding of the facts of spiritual life and growth, should be a top priority for disciples of Jesus, particularly those who work in the various fields of psychology and who consider it an intellectual and practical discipline. No understanding of the human self can be theoretically or practically adequate if it does not deal with the spiritual life.

Of course, spiritual formation in the second moment only

works because of the third and final moment: formation *by* the Spirit of God in Christ. This comes initially and mainly through immersion in and constant application of (John 8:31; 15:7) the *Word* of Christ, his gospel, and his commands that are inseparable from his person and his presence: "The words that I have spoken to you," he said, "are spirit and life" (John 6:63). And it is the movement of the Spirit in the spiritual formation of the individual personality that transforms the roots of behavior throughout the soul and body of the believer. This goes beyond simply hearing and receiving this word. Thus, when we have put on the new person— and we must *act* to do this, as it will not be done for us—we find the outflow of Christ's character from us to be, after all, the fruit of the Spirit.

The movements of the Spirit of Christ in the embodied personality are often identifiable, tangible events. Frequently they come in the form of individualized "words" from Christ to his apprentices who are involved in Kingdom living. He is our living teacher, and we are not asleep while we walk with him. Spiritual formation in Christ is not simply an unconscious process in which *results* may be observed while the One who works in us remains hidden. We actually experience his workings. We *look* for them, expect them, give thanks for them. We are consciously engaged with him in the details of our existence and our spiritual transformation.

However, it is not the immediacy of such experiences that tells us that it is the Spirit of God in Christ by whom we are being formed. Rather, the proof, if not the comfort, lies in the person we become and the deeds that flow from us. The tree is known by its fruit. When the Spirit who forms us causes us to love Jesus Christ above all and to walk in his example and deeds (1 Peter 2:21–23), when it upholds us in *obedience*, then we know that he is the Spirit by which we are formed (2 Corinthians 3:17). And with this knowledge as our framework, we may also take comfort in the immediate feeling of the movements of the Spirit in our personalities, lives, and surroundings.

Spiritual formation in Christ is accomplished, and the Great Commission fulfilled, as the regenerate soul makes its highest intent to live in the commandments of Christ and accordingly makes realistic plans to realize this intent by an adequate course of spiritual disciplines. Of course, no one can achieve this goal by themselves, but no one *has* to. God gives us others to share the pilgrimage, and we will be met by Christ in every step of the way. "Look, I am with you every instant," is what Jesus said, and it is also what he is doing.

We must stop using the fact that we cannot *earn* grace (whether for justification or for sanctification) as an excuse for not energetically seeking to *receive* grace. Having been found by God, we then become seekers of ever-fuller life in him. Grace is opposed to earning, but not to effort. The realities of Christian spiritual formation are that we will not be transformed "into his likeness" by more information, or by infusions, inspirations, or ministrations alone. Though all of these have an important place, they never suffice, and reliance upon them alone explains the now-common failure of committed Christians to rise much above a certain level of decency.

At the core of the human being is will, spirit, and heart. This core is reshaped, opening out to the reshaping of the whole life, only by *engagement*. First, engagement is to act with Christ in his example and his commands: "If you love me, you will keep my commandments," he said, "and I will ask the Father, and he will give you another srengthener, to be with you forever. This is the Spirit of truth" (John 14:15–17). The engagement must come first, followed by the helper insofar as obedience is concerned; as we try, fail, and learn, we engage with the spiritual disciplines. We add whole-life training to trying. We recognize that religious business-as-usual, the recommended routine for a "good" church member, is not enough to meet the need of the human soul. The problem of life is too radical for that to be the solution. We enter into activities that are more suited to our actual life condition and that are adequate to transform the whole self under grace, allowing the intention to live the commands of Christ to pass from will to deed.

Christian spiritual formation understood in this way is automatically ecumenical and inclusive in the sense that those thus formed, those who live in obedience to Christ, are thereby united and stand out as the same in their obedience. The substance of obedience is the only thing that can overcome the divisions imposed by encrusted differences in doctrine, ritual, and heritage. The lamp that is aglow in the obedient life *will* shine. The city set on the hill *cannot* be hid. Obedience to Christ from the heart and by the Spirit is such a radical reality that those who live in it automatically realize the unity that can never be achieved by direct efforts at union. It is not achieved by effort, but by who we *are:* "I am a companion of all who fear you" (Psalm 119:63).

Some years ago, ecumenism attempted to center on the confession of Christ as Lord. Little came of it because, in the manner to which we have been accustomed by history, the attitudes and actions of real life were left untouched by such a profession. But actual obedience to Christ as Lord would transform ordinary life entirely and bring those disciples who are walking with Christ together wherever their lives touch. Christians who are together in the natural contexts of life would immediately identify with one another because of the radically different kind of life, the eternal kind of life, manifestly flowing in them. Their mere non-cooperation with the evil around them would draw them together as magnet and iron. Any other differences would have no significance within the unity of obedience to the Christ who is present in his people.

Now, unfortunately, the other differences (cultural, social, denominational, and even personal) are the ones that govern the disunity of those who nevertheless identify themselves as Christians. Usually the power of these differences is tangibly at work when professing Christians from different groups are together. I cannot really imagine that this disunity would continue if all were centered in actual obedience to Christ. Set the clear intention and implementation on this aim, and all else follows. Without that, what else really matters? Heaven matters, of course, and attaining it surely does not depend upon attaining maturity in Christ. But to plan on that as a course of action, or to teach it as the normal Christian pattern, is quite another matter, one hardly to be recommended by anyone who actually has confidence in Christ.

The proper Christian *exclusiveness* will also be largely taken care of, I believe, by Christian spiritual formation centered on obedience to Christ from transformed personality. This will have the exclusiveness of the "God who answers by fire." Let the other spiritualities be equal to that which flowers into obedience to Christ if they can, and let the others themselves be the judges. "Their rock is not like our Rock, our enemies being the judge" (Deuteronomy 32:31).

The real issue relating to exclusiveness is whether the Christian actually has a relationship with God, a presence of God, that non-Christians do not have. Apart from Christian spiritual formation as described here, I believe there is little value in claiming exclusiveness for the Christian way.

The realization of this may be what is reflected in the current mass abandonment of the exclusiveness of Christianity that is going on among Western Christians now, especially in its academic centers. Why should one insist on the exclusiveness of Christianity if all it is is one more cultural form? But let the reality of Christian spiritual formation come to its fullness, and exclusiveness will take care of itself. If the witch and the warlock, the Buddhist and the Muslim, can truly walk in a holiness and power equal to that of Jesus Christ and his devoted followers, there is nothing more to say. But Christ himself, and not Christianity as a form of human culture, is the standard by which "we" as well as "they" are to be measured (Acts 17:31).

Perhaps this auspicious occasion in the life of a leading evangelical training center is an opportunity for us to ask ourselves, Are we seriously and realistically about the business of Christian spiritual formation as measured by unqualified love of Jesus Christ, and as specified by our "job description" in the Great Commission? How does our work, what we *really* do, actually relate to the charge he has left us? How much of what goes on in ourselves, our local assemblies, our denominations, and our schools, is dictated only by "futile ways inherited from [our] ancestors" (1 Peter 1:18)?

Suppose we were to engage in ground-zero planning, planning which, armed with the best theological and psychological understanding, considers only the aim without attempting to salvage or justify what is already in place through previous efforts. How much of what we do would be omitted? And how much of what we now omit would be done, if *all* we were trying to do was to bring our selves and others "to do all things whatsoever I have commanded you"? This question is surely put to each of us individually, as well as to all our institutions and programs, by the one who said, "Why do you call me 'Lord, Lord,' and do not do what I tell you?" (Luke 6:46).[3]

CHAPTER 8

The Spirit Is Willing, But . . .

The Body as a Tool for
Spiritual Growth

S PIRITUAL FORMATION is the process through which those who love and trust Jesus Christ effectively take on his character. When this process is what it should be, they increasingly live their lives as he would if he were in their place. Their outward conformity to his example and his instructions rises toward fullness as their inward sources of action take on the same character as his. They come more and more to share his vision, love, hope, feelings, and habits.

This process of "conformation to Christ," as we might more appropriately call it, is constantly supported by grace and otherwise would be impossible. But it is not therefore passive. Grace is opposed to *earning*, not to effort. In fact, nothing inspires and enhances effort like the experience of grace.

Yet it is today necessary to assert boldly and often that *becoming Christ-like never occurs without intense and well-informed action on our part.* This in turn cannot be reliably sustained outside of a like-minded fellowship. Our churches will be centers of spiritual formation only as they understand Christ-likeness and communicate it to individuals, through teaching and example, in a convincing and supportive fashion.

The Body and the Spiritual Life

Probably the least understood aspect of progress in Christ-likeness is *the role of the body in the spiritual life.*

Almost all of us are acutely aware of how the incessant clamorings of our bodies defeat our intentions to "be spiritual." The Apostle Paul explains that "what the flesh desires is opposed to the Spirit, and what the Spirit desires is opposed to the flesh; for these are opposed to each other, to prevent you from doing what you want" (Galatians 5:17). And Jesus's words, "The spirit indeed is willing, but the flesh is weak" (Matthew 26:41), are generally accepted as a *final* verdict on what human life must be like until we escape the body through death.

On the other hand, if the body is simply *beyond* redemption, then ordinary life is too. Many Christians seem prepared to accept this—at least in practice. But then spiritual formation really becomes impossible. That would be a defeat of major proportions for Christ's cause and could never be reconciled with the call to godly *living* that both permeates the Bible from end to end and resonates with the deep-seated human need to live as one ought.

We are glad, then, to find scriptural teachings about the body and its flesh running directly contrary to the "hopeless" view. Jesus is the primary witness to the unity of flesh and spirit before God. Long before his entry into history, however, the Psalmist spoke of his body longing for God (Psalm 63:1), of his "heart and flesh sing[ing] for joy to the living God" (84:2), and he called upon all flesh to "bless his holy name forever and ever" (145:21).

The prophet Joel foresaw the time when God's Spirit would be poured out upon all flesh (Joel 2:28–29). That prophecy began to be fulfilled on the Day of Pentecost (Acts 2:16–21). Thus, the picture of the body and of the flesh found in the writings of Paul stands in the sharpest of contrasts with the hopeless view of the body. The body is presented as a temple inhabited by the Holy Spirit. It is not meant to be used in sinning, but is meant for the Lord, and "the Lord for the body" (1 Corinthians 6:13).

Through the power of God which raised Christ from the dead, Paul tells us, "your bodies are members of Christ" (1 Corinthians 6:15). Our bodies do not even belong to us, but have been bought by Christ, who gives them a life "from above" and opens the way for us "to glorify God in [our bodies]" (1 Corinthians 6:20). Thus, we can "present [our] bodies as a living sacrifice, holy and acceptable to God," this being our "spiritual worship" (Romans 12:1).

Human Nature

In order to understand the role of the body—both negative and positive—in the spiritual life, and in life generally, we must take a deeper view of the nature of human personality, character, and action.

Each of us grows up in surroundings that train us to speak, think, feel, and act like others around us. "Monkey see, monkey do," goes the proverb. This is the mechanism by which human personality is formed, and it is largely for the good. But it also embeds in us habits of evil that permeate all human life. Humanly standard patterns of responding to the "cravings of sinful man, the lust of his eyes and the boasting of what he has and does," which the Apostle John said make up "the world" (1 John 2:16), seize upon little children through their participation in the lives of those around them. Sinful practices become their habits, *then* their choice, and finally their character.

The very language they learn to speak incorporates desecration of God and neighbor. They come to identify themselves and be identified by others through these practices. What is wrong and destructive is done without thinking about it. The wrong thing to do seems quite "natural," while the right thing to do becomes forced and unnatural at best—especially if done because it is right. You can observe this in almost any ten-year-old child acting freely with her peers or living in the family setting.

The New Testament texts normally use the word "flesh" to refer to the human body formed in the ways of evil and against God. Not that the human body as such, or even desires as such, are evil. They are God's good creations, and capable of serving and glorifying Him, as we have seen already. But when shaped in a life context of family, neighborhood, school, and work that is godless or anti-God, they constitute a pervasive structure of evil. Desire then becomes the "sinful passions . . . at work in our bodies" (Romans 7:5). Our very bodies are poised to sin, only awaiting the occasion. As God said to Cain in the ancient story, "Sin is lurking at the door; its desire is for you, but you must master it" (Genesis 4:7). The situation becomes so bad that Paul says, "nothing good dwells within me, that is, in my flesh" (Romans 7:18).

When we come to new life in Christ, our bodies and their deformed desire system do not automatically shift to the side of Christ, but continue to oppose him. Occasionally a remarkable change may occur, such as total relief from an addiction. But this is very infrequent, and it is *never* true that the habits of sin generally are displaced from our bodily parts and personality by the new birth.

James reminds us that "one is tempted by one's own desire, being lured and enticed by it; then, when that desire has conceived, it gives birth to sin, and that sin, when it is fully grown, gives birth to death" (James 1:14–15). Peter urges us, "as aliens and exiles to abstain from the desires of the flesh that wage war against the soul" (1 Peter 2:11). Paul tells us that if we live in terms of the flesh we will die: "But if by the Spirit you put to death the misdeeds of the body, you will live" (Romans 8:13). Elsewhere he cites himself as one who "punish[es] my body and enslave[s] it, so that after proclaiming to others I myself should not be disqualified" (1 Corinthians 9:27). And all of these statements concern Christians of long standing.

Christ-likeness Must Be Planned For

Admittedly, all of this sounds strange in today's religious context. It is a simple fact that nowadays the task of becoming Christ-like is rarely taken as a serious objective to be thoughtfully planned for, and the reality of our embodied personality dealt with accordingly. I have inquired before many church and parachurch groups regarding their plan for putting to death or *mortifying* "whatever belongs to your earthly nature" or flesh (see, for example, Colossians 3:5). I have *never once* had a positive response to this question. Indeed, mortifying or putting things to death doesn't seem to be the kind of thing today's Christians would be caught doing. Yet there it stands, at the center of the New Testament teachings.

When Jesus taught about discipleship, on the other hand, he made it very clear that one could not be the servant of the body and its demands and also succeed in his course of training. This is the meaning of what he said about denying ourselves, taking up our cross, about "losing our life" for his sake and the gospel's (Matthew 10:39; 16:24–26), and about "forsaking all" to follow him (Luke 14:25–35). It is the same theme that is struck by Paul:

"Those who belong to Christ Jesus have crucified the flesh with its passions and desires" (Galatians 5:24). He puts in contrast those who make a god of their belly (Romans 16:18; Philippians 3:19), the "belly" being the bodily center of desire.

Of course one cannot overcome the hardened patterns of desires by force of will alone. Rather, it is as we by faith place our bodily being in subordination to Christ that we experience a new presence in our members, moving them toward the good things of God and allowing the old bodily forces to recede into the background of life where they belong. Thus, it truly is "by the spirit" that we "put to death the misdeeds of the body." The natural desires, and my body itself, remain with me, of course, but now as servants of God and of my will to serve Him, not as my masters.

Our part in this transformation, in addition to constant faith and hope in Christ, is purposeful, strategic use of our bodies in ways that will retrain them, replacing the "motions of sin in our members" with the motions of Christ. This is how we take up our cross daily. It is how we submit our bodies, as a living sacrifice, how we offer the parts of our body to him as "instruments of righteousness" (Romans 6:13).

When Direct Effort Fails

Sometimes, of course, submission to God means just to do what pleases Him. Ultimately that is always our aim. But frequently we are unable to do this by *direct* effort. Often when we come to do the right thing we have *already* done the wrong thing, because that is what was sitting in our body "at the ready." Intention alone cannot suffice in most situations where we find ourselves. We must be "in shape." If not, trying will normally be too late, or totally absent. Instead, our intention and effort must be carried into effect by *training* which leaves our body *poised* to do what Christ would do, well before the occasion arises. Such training is supplied by the *disciplines for life in the Spirit.*

Now, a *discipline* is an activity in our power, which we pursue in order to become able to do what we cannot do by direct effort. Disciplines are required in every area of life, including the spiritual. Therefore, Jesus directed and led his disciples into disciplines for the spiritual life: fasting, prayer, solitude, silence, service, study, fellowship, and so forth.

For example, Jesus told his closest friends that they would run like scared rabbits when his enemies came to capture him. They emphatically and sincerely denied it. But the body has a life of its own which far outreaches what we know of ourselves. The readinesses actually in their bodies would not support their intention. Jesus, of course, knew this.

When he took Peter, James, and John into the Garden of Gethsemane to aid him in his struggle, they fell asleep. He awoke them and told them how they could succeed with their good intentions, which he never questioned. How were they going to die for him if they couldn't even stay awake with him for an hour? So he said, "Watch and pray that you may not come into the time of trial; the spirit indeed is willing, but the flesh is weak" (Matthew 26:41). He tried to help them understand how their bodies were influencing them and what they could do to keep them in line with their spirits. "Watching," or staying alert to what was happening, and praying with him, was something they could have done. Surely participation with Jesus in the awesome events of the Garden *would* have fortified them against failure to stand with him later. As it turned out, what was in their bodies and souls—fear of death and shame—remained unchallenged and their "temptation" did overwhelm them.

Quite generally, now, the teachings of Jesus are viewed as so "hard" only because our embodied personalities are formed *against* them. Take, for example, his teaching in Matthew 5:22, that we should not speak insultingly of or to others, calling them "fools" (i.e., "twerps," or worse). I have known many "faithful Christians" who use vile and contemptuous language on others who do not perform just right in a traffic, work, or even home setting. They say, "That's just me," or, "I can't help it."

Similarly, we can note the purposive, lustful stare that Jesus speaks of in Matthew 5:28, or the striking back by word or fist later on in this chapter, or the practicing of religion for human applause with which he deals in the next chapter. No law of nature forces the "easy" and disobedient response in these situations. It is just a habit embedded in our bodies and, of course, habits always produce powerful rationalizations for themselves.

Now suppose that we decided to learn how to do what Jesus says we should do in these cases. Suppose, for example, we wanted to train ourselves to bless and pray for anyone who does something in traffic that endangers or displeases us. Instead of calling such a one a fool or a stupid jerk or worse, we are going to use words of blessing and let our hearts go out in generous goodwill toward others. Could we do it? Of course we could, if we took appropriate steps. It is not a law of nature that makes us assassinate the humanity of others.

How We Can Change

And *how* would we do it? First, we begin by acknowledging the good of what we are going to do and asking God's assistance. Second, we begin to practice controlling our tongue. Not by trying not to insult people *when* they shake us up. No, we begin further back from the target situation. Possibly we step out of the realm of words by not speaking for a twenty-four-hour period—even by dwelling in silence with the TV and radio off. This probably will require that we go into solitude for the period of time.

Note that all of this is something we do with our bodies. We relocate and reorient our body in our world. We learn a new relation to our body—specifically, our ears and tongues. This pervasively impacts our minds, hearts, and souls, as it gives opportunity to explore our world in silence and find our proper place in it. This in turn allows us to gain insight into why we use the accustomed foul and insulting language.

Of course it is because it gives us a sense of power over the "jerk." It lies on a continuum with shooting him. That insight then opens up better ways of viewing what is actually going on in traffic or elsewhere—indeed in life. Suddenly we see what pathetic behavior our "exploding" is, and we discover attractive alternatives to it. We can even begin to develop the habit of blessing now, for we see the goodness of it and know that we are capable of silence, where we find God present. The words of James become very meaningful: everyone should be "quick to listen, slow to speak, [and] slow to anger" (James 1:19).

We enter into *each* of the teachings of Jesus by choosing different behaviors that are relevant, finding the space—making the arrangements—in our lives to put them into action, and re-visioning the situation in the new behavioral space that includes God. The interaction between new uses of the body and inward re-positioning toward the context is essential. Learning to do what he taught is not just a mental shift without assistance from a modified use of the body, for behavior and life are not mental.

The lustful look also is bodily behavior and based on bodily behavior. We choose to be in position and posture to engage in it. Millions of people say they cannot stop it, just like those who rationalize their verbal assaults on others. But it is, in fact, only a habit of self-indulgence. It can easily be broken when that is earnestly wanted. You do not have to look at the bodily parts of others, and you can train your thoughts away from lusting if you cultivate chaste habits of thought and attitudes. Appropriate disciplines of study, meditation, and service, for example, can break the action of looking to lust, as many have established by experience. Here too the use and training of the body is the place where faith meets grace to achieve conformity to Christ.

What we find, then, is that the body is the place of our *direct* power. It is the little "power pack" that God has assigned to us as the field of our freedom and development. Our lives depend upon our direction and management of them. But the body can acquire a "life of its own"—tendencies to behave without regard to our conscious intentions. In our fallen world this life is prepossessed by evil, so that we do not have to *think* to do what is wrong, but *must* think and plan and practice—and receive grace—if we are to succeed in doing what is right.

But Christ shows us how to bring the body from opposition to support of the new life he gives us, "the Spirit" now in us. He calls us to share his *practices* in sustaining his own relationship to the Father. Indeed, these practices—of solitude, silence, study, service, prayer, worship—are now the places where we arrange to meet regularly with him and his Father to be his students or disciples in Kingdom living.

Some may think it strange that such practices, the disciplines for life in the Spirit, are all bodily behaviors. But it cannot be otherwise. Learning Christ-likeness is not passive. It is active engagement with and in God. And we act with our bodies. Moreover, this bodily engagement is what lays the foundation in our bodily members for readinesses for holiness, and increasingly removes the readinesses to sin—so that "Christ will be exalted now as always in my body, whether by life or by death. For to me, living is Christ and dying is gain" (Philippians 1:20–21).

Further Reading

Foster, R. *Celebration of Discipline,* rev. ed. (Harper & Row, 1988). A contemporary classic on the disciplines for the spiritual life.

McGuire, M. "Religion and the Body: Rematerializing the Human Body in the Social Sciences of Religion." *Journal for the Scientific Study of Religion* 29 (1990): 283–96. An excellent entrée into philosophical and academic interpretations of the body's role in personality, with bibliography.

Taylor, J. *Holy Living and Holy Dying,* Classics of Western Spirituality series (Paulist, 1992). Many other editions. Practical directions on the use of the body for spiritual growth by a great Christian of the sixteenth century.

Willard, D. *The Spirit of the Disciplines* (Harper & Row, 1988). Especially chapters 1 through 7, which deal with basic points in a theology and soteriology of the body.

CHAPTER 9

Living in the Vision of God

Whoever serves me must follow me, and where I am, there will my servant be also. Whoever serves me, the Father will honor.

—Jesus (John 12:26)

WHEN YOU GO TO ASSISI, you will find many people who talk a great deal about St. Francis, many monuments to him, and many businesses thriving by selling memorabilia of him. But you will not find anyone who carries in himself the *fire* that Francis carried. No doubt many fine folks are there, but they do not have the character of Francis, nor do they do the deeds of Francis, nor have his effects.

What is true in this case is not peculiar to it. Rather, this is simply one of the more obvious illustrations of a general tendency of human life—and of the spiritual life as well. It happens in the professional world, the world of business, of government, education, and the arts: A person of some great inspiration and ability emerges and rises far above his or her origins and surroundings. Perhaps it is a King David of Israel, a Socrates, a St. Anthony or St. Francis, a Martin Luther or a George Fox or a John Wesley. In each of these people there is a . . . well, a "certain something."

They really *are* different, and that difference explains why these individuals have such great effect, and why movements and institutions grow up around them. It is as if they stand in another world, and from there they have extraordinary effects in this world—as God acts with them. Organization of their activities takes place, and other organizations spin off from them as numbers of talented individuals are drawn to them and make their lives in their wake. But these other individuals—usually, but not always, very well-intending—do not carry the "fire," the "certain something," within them. The mission or missions that have been set afoot begin a subtle divergence from the vision that gripped the founder, and before too long the institution and its mission has become the vision.

This happens in secular settings as well. Arthur Andersen was a man of rock-solid integrity, with a crystal-clear vision of accounting as a profession. He built a magnificent accounting firm on strong moral principles. But eventually the people who ran the firm became obsessed with moneymaking and success, and then with helping clients make money and be successful, instead of holding those clients responsible ("account-able") to the public goods they all professed to serve. These people—who acted in the good name of Arthur Andersen, but without his vision—brought disaster upon themselves and upon thousands of unsuspecting people who depended upon them. Had the moral fire burned in them that burned in Arthur Andersen, that would not have happened. But a false fire of greed and ambition burned in its place. The cuckold of "success" laid its eggs in the nest of service-to-the-public-good, and a monster was hatched that destroyed the nest and all in it.

St. Francis and Arthur Andersen are among the more glamorous and notorious illustrations of a hard reality. In most cases, when the original fire dies out, the associated institutions and individuals carry on for a while, increasingly concerned about success and survival, and then either they find another basis to stand upon, or they simply disappear. (Consider the case of Charles Finney and Oberlin College, which he founded, or any number of other originally Christian colleges and universities.)

While the process seen here is not restricted to religious movements, it is especially obvious and painful to behold in their case. There is a real point to saying that in religious matters, *nothing fails like success.* These types of movements touch the human heart very deeply and serve profound human needs. Because of this, they soon attract many who do not even *want* the fire of the founder—they do not really understand it. But they do need and like the light and the warmth it provides. Eventually, however, and without consciously intending to do so, they extinguish the very fire that provides the light and warmth, or it simply dies out from lack of being tended. Then an operation may continue under the name, trading in memorabilia. But it isn't the same operation on the inside, and truthfully its effects are not the same.

Thus "apostasy" (standing away from) is in fact a natural and fairly normal process in life. It is what should be expected, not something to be surprised about. It would be remarkable and abnormal if it did not happen. It is never, primarily, a failure of belief or correct doctrine, or a conscious decision. It is a subtle shifting of vision, of feeling and will—of how people see things and feel about things, especially about themselves and what they are doing. The shifts in belief and the conscious decisions are only the *epicenter* of the "soulquake." They lie at the surface of life. The *center* lies miles deep in the soul of the individuals involved.

The soulquake may be something that happens *within* the lifetime of individuals, as in the cases of biblical kings such as Saul, Amaziah, and Uzziah, or many individuals that have come to public attention in recent years. Or it may occur across a few generations—rarely more than a few—as with the degeneration of the kingship in Israel from David, through Solomon, to Rehoboam.

A well-known contemporary teacher of ministers has remarked that *few ministers finish well.* This statement is even more true of ministries than it is of ministers—who, I suspect, do better on the whole than appears to be the case. Unfortunately, on the other hand, nearly every denomination one could name vividly illustrates the process under discussion here, as do many educational and charitable organizations.

But what is the fine texture of the underlying change that reveals itself in the loss of the inward fire of vision to the outward accretions of mission or ministry? The central point lies in a fact noted by Henri Nouwen: *nothing conflicts with the love of Christ like service to Christ.* What a strange thing to say! Perhaps it is an overstatement. But it is true that well-meaning service *to* God has a very strong tendency to undermine the kind of vision of God that fuels greatness *for* God in the human scene. With the possible exception of David, who indeed finished well, we see this constantly in the kings of Judah and Israel.

Uzziah's case is especially instructive: "But when he had become strong, his heart was so lifted up that he acted corruptly. For he was false to the Lord his God, and entered the temple of the Lord to make offering on the altar of incense" (2 Chronicles 26:16). Uzziah became strong through his devotion to the Lord. For much of his life he focused upon knowing God in a close relationship. "He did what was right in the sight of the Lord. . . . He set himself to seek God in the days of Zechariah, who instructed him in the fear of God; and as long as he sought the Lord, God made him prosper" (2 Chronicles 26:4–5).

But the works that were accomplished through Uzziah's association with God in action distracted him from his original vision and refocused him on himself and what he was doing. "His heart was lifted up." This language of the Bible became a standard way of diagnosing the failure of the kings of Judah and Israel. It always had the result that they *took more upon themselves than was warranted.* In Uzziah's case, it was his decision to perform temple rituals that were not permitted to him. But in most cases these kings formed human alliances or tried to establish practices that overestimated what could be accomplished by human strength. They glorified themselves and did not rely upon God.

Because they became wrongly focused, they could not live in the lesson of the prophet Jahaziel: "Do not fear or be dismayed at this great multitude; for the battle is not yours but God's. . . . This battle is not for you to fight; take your position, stand still, and see the victory of the Lord on your behalf. . . . Do not fear or be dismayed . . . the Lord will be with you" (2 Chronicles 20:15–17).

What, then, is the general pattern? Intense devotion to God by the individual or group brings substantial outward success. Outward success brings a sense of accomplishment and a sense of responsibility for what has been achieved—and for *further* achievement. For onlookers the outward success is the whole thing. The sense of accomplishment and responsibility reorients vision away from God to what we are doing and are to do—usually to the applause and support of sympathetic people. The mission increasingly *becomes* the vision. It becomes what we are focused upon. The mission and ministry is what we spend our thoughts, feelings, and strength upon. Goals occupy the place of the vision of God in the inward life, and we find ourselves caught up in a visionless pursuit of various goals. Grinding it out.

This is the point at which service to Christ replaces love for Christ. The inward reality of love for God, and absorption in what

He is doing, is no longer the center of the life, and may even become despised, or at least is disregarded. "No time for that" becomes the governing attitude, no matter what we may say. The fire of God in the human soul will always look foolish to those who like its effects but do not understand where those effects come from.

At this point a pervasive consciousness of one's rights and perks may set in. Amaziah, who had been a fairly good king in Judah, defeated the Edomites—and brought their gods to Jerusalem and worshiped them! When rebuked by a prophet, he said, "Have we made you a royal counselor? Stop! Why should you be put to death?" (2 Chronicles 25:16).

Very often it is not the founders but those who gather about them who insist on the perks and rights. Often they see that as a way of serving the one they admire, and perhaps they are convinced that the founder is not an ordinary human being. David, when thirsty on the field of battle, made an offhand remark about wanting a drink from the deep well by the gate in Bethlehem. Three of his "mighty men" overheard his remark and broke through enemy lines to bring him the water. But he would not drink it. He "poured it out to the Lord," because their devotion had made it too precious for him to drink (2 Samuel 23:16). This is a most illuminating insight into the good and humble heart of David, seen on many other occasions in his life. It shows how he saw himself in God's world.

St. Francis also provides many illustrations of this type of enduring humility. But in his case it proved too much for his "order" to follow, and within a few years he was in a struggle with his followers because the regulations he proposed for them (the "rule") were too lowly for them. He lost. He even became an object of derision among some of his earliest associates because of the fire that burned within him.

As we have just noted, such a departure from the founder may be accompanied by assumptions to the effect that he or she is in some sense not "normal," not "flesh and blood"—whereas in fact it is their very "normalcy," and their acute awareness of it, that leads them to adopt the measures they do to keep themselves centered on God—to keep the vision right and bright. They, and not their followers, understand the inward battle that has to be fought. Their followers often rely upon the assumption that the founder, or leader, is "unusual" or "abnormally gifted" to relieve themselves of the burden of genuinely being like him or her. This is usually firmed up by a total lack of understanding of how the leaders came to have the vision of God they do—and sometime the leaders are not clear about this either.

So we can summarize the process by which the mission and its goals replace the original vision as the ultimate point of reference for the people involved. Vision of God and of oneself in God inspires a combination of humility and great aspiration for God. This combination leads to remarkable efforts in dependence upon God. Great effects are achieved because God acts *with* efforts made in dependence upon him and for his sake. *The effects take on a life of their own.* Surrounding people see nothing but the effects, which indeed *are* very remarkable and worthy of support. Sometimes the human support may also be of God. But the effects of all this have to be carefully watched, to prevent them from corrupting the heart away from an appropriate vision of God and the humble valor flowing therefrom.

King Solomon began well. He knew about God at least, from his association with his father David, and he understood he could not carry out his work by himself. He prayed for wisdom and knowledge. God gave it to him. He became very great (2 Chronicles 9). But to strengthen his position he formed alliances through marriage with royalty of many nations, and his seven hundred wives turned his heart away from Jehovah to worship their gods

(1 Kings 11:1–6). By the time he died, he had evolved a government that was bitterly oppressive, with the people ready to rebel, and he had a son to rule after him who was a fool. It is not unreasonable to think that what really happened to Solomon was a building program.

———————

But does this have to happen? Is it simply unavoidable? The answer is, in general, "No." Some individuals manage to avoid it, though many do not. And some groups or organizations have long postponed it. The early Christians hold the record for sustaining the inward fire of vision in the "founders." For two or three centuries, it seems, the vision of Jesus Christ as Lord burned brightly in their hearts. The tremendous successes of the movement only very slowly generated an outward "vessel" that replaced the treasure of Christ as the center of attention and devotion in their lives.

The earliest generations of Christians were remarkably successful in passing the sacred vision that positioned and guarded them in life on to the next generation. It was not an entirely new phenomenon. In the Old Testament, Joshua (Exodus 33:11) and Elisha (2 Kings 2:9) were two cases where the disciple sought the Lord as did their masters (Moses and Elijah), and as a result carried on through their lives in the same spirit.

In later Christian history, we find clear examples of the transgenerational sharing of the original fire in the Jesuits, the Quakers, the Moravian Brethren, and the Methodists. No doubt there are many other cases not so well known. So it can be done. And there are many cases of individuals in each generation who have finished well. What is essentially involved?

The answer is simple in concept, but obviously it is not easy in execution—and especially for the transgenerational case. It is a matter of *identifying and sustaining the sense or vision of God, self, and world that pervaded and animated the originators.* One cannot write a recipe for this, for it is a highly personal matter, permitting of much individual variation and freedom. It also is dependent upon grace—that is, upon God acting in our lives to accomplish what we cannot accomplish on our own.

All of this acknowledged, there are things any person can do—and must do—to receive and sustain the inner spiritual fire that keeps mission and ministry in its proper place, preventing them from becoming the limiting vision that obsesses us and eventually strangles us.

The first thing is to heartily acknowledge the practical inevitability of the loss of vision. The acknowledgment must be something that is explicit and regular. One need not become paranoid about it, just honest. One must find ways of keeping it before oneself and one's associates without becoming a bore. Creativity and good taste are to be used.

Second, we must identify, understand, and adhere to the founding vision. This is not easy. Even the founders themselves may not be clear about exactly what moved them and how they came to be the persons they are. Often a commendable modesty and humility prevents them from inquiring very deeply into their own lives, and certainly from "imposing" what they find there upon others. But, while this attitude is commendable, it has the built-in handicap of making it very difficult to sustain the vision, in oneself and in others. So one must be honest, thorough, and explicit about what the vision was—and what it must now be. The focus must be on the vision, not upon the individuals who have it, even though it must be the individuals who bear the vision and carry out the mission.

Third, steps must be taken to live in the central content of the vision. The wisdom of Proverbs tells us, "Trust in the Lord with all your heart, and don't place your faith in your own understanding. Acknowledge God in all you do, and he will smooth your pathway. Don't think *you* have got it figured out" (3:5–7). And again: "Watch over your heart with all diligence, for what is in your heart will determine what your life amounts to (4:23).

At the center of care for the heart is the love of God. This must be the joyful aim of our life. That is why Jesus, underlining the deep understanding of life worked out through the Jewish experience, stated that the first commandment is to "love the Lord your God with all your heart, and with all your soul, and with all your mind, and with all your strength" (Mark 12:30). This is a command. It is something we are to do, and something we *can* do. We *will* learn how to do it *if we intend* to do it. God will help us, and we will find a way.

The love of God, and only the love of God, secures the vision of God, keeps God constantly before our mind. Thomas Watson tells us that "the first fruit of love is *the musing of the mind upon God*. He who is in love, his thoughts are ever upon the object. He who loves God is ravished and transported with the contemplation of God. . . . God is the treasure, and where the treasure is, there is the heart." King David gives us the secret of his life: "I keep the Lord always before me; because he is at my right hand, I shall not be moved" (Psalm 16:8).

Vision of God secures humility. Seeing God for who He is enables us to see ourselves for who we are. This makes us *bold,* for we see clearly what great good and evil are at issue, and we see that it is not up to us to accomplish it, but up to God—who is more than able. We are delivered from pretending, from being presumptuous about ourselves, and from pushing as if the outcome depended on us. We persist without frustration, and we practice calm and joyful noncompliance with evil of any kind.

God looks to those who are humble and contrite of spirit and who tremble when he speaks (Isaiah 66:2). He resists the proud, but gives grace to the humble (1 Peter 5:5). Remember, grace means that he is acting in their lives.

So the humble are dependent upon God, not on themselves. They humble themselves "under the mighty hand of God" (1 Peter 5:6)—that is, by depending upon God to act. They abandon outcomes entirely to him. They "cast all [their] anxiety on him, because he cares for [them]" (1 Peter 5:7). The result is assurance that the mission and the ministry will be accomplished, in God's time and in God's way. *They* don't need to be the vision, and the goals we set for them are God's business, not ours. We do the very best we know, we work hard, and even self-sacrificially. But *we do not carry the load,* and *our ego is not involved* in any way with the mission and the ministry. In our love of Jesus and his Father, we truly have abandoned our life to him. Our life is not an object of deep concern.

In order to sustain and develop such a life of loving abandonment to God, an overall plan of life is required, incorporating special practices that care for the inner person. These are the familiar disciplines for spiritual life. We cannot discuss these here, but the next step forward for those persons who have decided that they will love God with all their heart, soul, mind, and strength is to put in place those regular practices that will make it possible. This will take some time, and it will require study, experimentation, and guidance by the Holy Spirit. But it can be done, and when it is done, life becomes incalculably easier, sweeter, and stronger. Mission and ministry are no longer burdensome, though they may be quite challenging and strenuous. His yoke is, nonetheless, easy, and his burden is light, and there is rest in the soul (Matthew 11:29–30).

For those who have known this in the past, the call is to return to the first love and do the first works, and then learn how to develop that first position into the life we are now living. For those who have never known it, the call is to focus on the love of God for us until our heart, soul, mind, and strength overflow with love in return. "We love him because he first loved us" (1 John 4:19).

And for those who, standing in the love of God, are concerned about the next generation around them, and about their entry into the full vision of the God of love, the call is to make these matters a subject of serious and prolonged discussion and prayer with those who will lead into the future. Talk openly, regularly, honestly, and lovingly.

Eventually judgments must be made as to who will be entrusted with the future of the organization. These must be made lovingly but firmly, and "under the mighty hand of God." They cannot be avoided. What we can do is prepare for them by intelligent, biblical, and constant teaching and practice, by word and by example. And in this matter too we have to rely upon the action of God in our midst (grace)—God, whom we love, and whose love we constantly commend to others.

Everything comes down to actually loving God with all our heart, soul, mind, and strength and to making foremost in our plans those activities that will meet the active grace of God to let that love be our life.

CHAPTER 10

Idaho Springs Inquiries Concerning Spiritual Formation

IN THE FALL OF 1999 a small group of Christian teachers gathered in retreat near Idaho Springs, Colorado, to reflect prayerfully on the meaning and prospects of Christian spiritual formation today. With no human authority, but a deep concern for the life of Jesus Christ in his people now and for the worldwide understanding of his gospel, we sought clear and helpful responses to several questions about spiritual formation that now confront us. The following responses to those questions are formulated by me and may not be exactly what others from the group would say. But my hope is that they might serve to direct us in meeting the challenges of our day to profoundly Christ-like being and living and in gaining maximum benefit for the church from the upsurge of interest in spiritual formation that characterizes the end of the twentieth century and the beginning of the twenty-first.

What is spiritual formation? How is it to be described in the language of contemporary life?

There is a hidden dimension to every human life, one not visible to others or fully graspable even by ourselves. This is God's gift to us in creation, that we might have the space to become the persons we choose to be. From here we manage our lives as best we can, utilizing whatever resources of understanding, emotion, and circumstance are available. It is here we stand before God and our conscience. This hidden dimension of the self is commonly thought of in spatial terms—as the "within" or "insides" or "depth" of the person or self. Such language expresses the fact that it is hidden and that it is foundational. The heart, soul, mind, feelings, and intentions lie in this area, and these make up the true character of the person: who that person is and what they can be counted on to do.

Within the invisible dimension of the person, and right at its conscious center, lies the *human* spirit. "God is Spirit," the creative will that creates and governs the universe, and "spirit" is the creative element in human nature, the "image of God in man." The human spirit is primarily what we today call "will," the capacity of choice and resolution, and what biblically and traditionally is called "heart." It is the radical source of our life: of the stream of actions and influences and contributions we make to our shared, visible world and its history.

Spiritual formation, without regard to any specifically religious context or tradition, is *the process by which the human spirit or will is given a definite form, or character.* Make no mistake, it is a process that happens to *everyone.* The most despicable as well as the most admirable of persons have had a spiritual formation. Their spirits or hearts have been formed. We all become a certain kind of person, gain a specific character, and that is the outcome of a process of spiritual formation understood in general human terms. Fortunate or blessed are those who are able to find or are given a path of life that will form their spirit and inner world in a way that is truly strong and good.

Christian spiritual formation, in contrast, is *the redemptive process of forming the inner human world so that it takes on the character of the inner being of Christ himself.* In the degree to which it is successful, the outer life of the individual becomes a natural expression or outflow of the character and teachings of Jesus. But the external manifestation of Christ-likeness is not the focus of the process, and when it is made the main emphasis the process will be defeated, falling into crushing legalisms and parochialisms. "Until Christ is formed in you" (Galatians 4:19) is the eternal watchword of Christian spiritual formation, fortified by the assurance that "the letter [of the law] kills, but the spirit of the law gives life" (2 Corinthians 3:6).

Thus, for example, Jesus's teachings in the Sermon on the Mount (Matthew 5–7) make reference to various behaviors: acting out anger, looking to lust, heartless divorce, verbal manipulation, returning evil for evil, and so forth. But as abundant experience now teaches, to strive merely to *act* in conformity with these illustrations of what living from the Kingdom of God is like is to attempt the impossible, and also will lead to doing things that are obviously wrong and even ridiculous. It would merely increase "the 'righteousness' of the scribe and pharisee," not to "go beyond" it to find genuine transformation of who I am as Christ's man or woman in his Kingdom (Matthew 5:20).

The instrumentalities of Christian spiritual formation (which we will usually mean from here on when we speak simply of "spiritual formation") involve much more than human effort. Well-informed human effort is necessary, for spiritual formation is not a passive process. But Christ-likeness of the inner being is not a merely human attainment. It is, finally, a gift of grace. The resources for it are not human, but come from the interactive presence of the Holy Spirit in the lives of those who place their confidence in Christ, as well as from the spiritual treasures stored in the body of Christ's people upon the earth. Therefore it is not only formation of the spirit or inner being of the individual that we have in mind, but also formation *by* the Spirit of God and by the spiritual riches of Christ's continuing incarnation in his people, past and present—including, most prominently, the treasures of his written and spoken word.

What are the primary elements or activities involved in an effective process of Christian spiritual formation?

There is first of all the action of the Holy Spirit and the Word of the gospel that awakens those "dead in trespasses and sins" to the love of God and to the availability of life in His Kingdom through confidence in Jesus Christ. This makes possible their acceptance of Christ as Savior, which then opens their souls to the influx of divine life, making them "participants of the divine nature" (2 Peter 1:4) and in that sense children of God. The initiative of the Spirit, of the Word, and of those who in various ways minister the Spirit and the Word never ceases in the process of spiritual formation.

But there is also a constant seeking on the part of the individual disciple and of groups of disciples. "When you search for me, you will find me," the prophetic word is, "if you seek me with all your heart" (Jeremiah 29:13). And again: "He rewards those who seek him" (Hebrews 11:6). This seeking is driven by the desire to be inwardly pure before God, to be wholly for Him, to love Him with all our heart, soul, mind, and strength. Inseparable from that desire is the desire to be good as Christ himself is good: to love our relatives, friends, and neighbors as he loves them, and to serve them with the powers of God's Kingdom.

This seeking is implemented through the discovery of the state of our own heart and inner world by study, reflection, prayer, and counsel, and then through the taking of appropriate measures to change what is not right within, as well as in the visible, social world of which we are a part. We find what God is doing in us and in the visible world and merge our actions into His. This is what Jesus described as constantly seeking "first for the kingdom of God and his kind of righteousness" (Matthew 6:33).

Most of the activities commonly identified as "religious" activities *can* be a part of the process of spiritual formation, and should be. Public and private worship, study of scripture, nature, and God's acts in human history, prayer, giving to godly causes, and service to others can all be highly effective elements in spiritual formation. But they must be thoughtfully and resolutely approached for that purpose, or they will have little or no effect in promoting it.

Other less commonly practiced activities, such as fasting, solitude, silence, listening prayer, scripture memorization, frugal living, confession, journaling, submission to the will of others as appropriate, and well-used spiritual direction, are in fact more foundational for spiritual formation in Christ-likeness than the better-known religious practices and are essential for their profitable use.

All such activities must be seen in the context of an intimate, personal walk with Jesus himself as our constant Savior and Teacher. No formula can be written for spiritual formation, for it is a dynamic relationship and one that is highly individualized. One can be sure, however, that any God-blessed undertaking of spiritual formation will include much of what has just been mentioned here.

How is spiritual formation expressed in the language of the Bible? Is it a biblical concept? And is there anything really new in the current usage, or is it just new language for something we have been doing all along?

It is a biblical concept, expressed in many ways in the Bible—in admonition, in prayer, in teaching, in example. "Keep my words within your heart," Proverbs says, "for they are life to those who find them, and healing to all their flesh. Keep your heart with all vigilance, for from it flow the springs of life" (Proverbs 4:21–23). The Psalmist cries, "Create in me a clean heart, O God, and put a new and right spirit within me. . . . Sustain in me a willing spirit. . . . The sacrifice acceptable to God is a broken spirit; a broken and contrite heart, O God, you will not despise" (Psalm 51:10–17; see also Isaiah 66:2–6). Later, a strategy of spiritual formation is indicated: "I treasure your word in my heart, so that I may not sin against you" (Psalm 119:11; see also Joshua 1:8 and Psalm 1).

God considers what is in the heart (1 Samuel 16:7), seeks those who would worship him in spirit and in truth, and can only be worshiped by such people (John 4:23–24). He speaks a word so penetrating that it can differentiate between what is soul and what is spirit in the human being (Hebrews 4:12). He identifies and rejects those who honor him with their lips but have hearts that are far from him (Isaiah 29:13; see also Matthew 15:8–9, 18).

Biblical religion is above all a religion of the heart and of the keeping of the heart. Thus, Jesus himself stresses that there is no good tree that produces bad fruit, nor a bad tree that produces good fruit (Luke 6:43), and that the good and the evil that come out of people come from their hearts (Luke 6:45; Mark 7:21–23). We are to clean, not the outside, but the inside of the cup, and the outside will take care of itself (Matthew 23:25–26).

The Apostle Paul's constant instruction is for us to renovate our inner being by "putting off the old person" and "putting on the new person," characterized by "compassion, kindness, humility, meekness, and patience . . . ; just as the Lord has forgiven you, so you also must forgive. Above all, clothe yourselves with love, which binds everything together in perfect harmony" (Colossians 3:12–14). He prays that the Ephesians would be "strengthened in your inner being with power through his Spirit, and that Christ may dwell in your hearts through faith, . . . so that you may be filled with all the fullness of God" (Ephesians 3:16–19); and he testifies that his own "inner nature is being renewed day by day, . . . because we look not at what can be seen but at what cannot be seen" (2 Corinthians 4:16–18).

Thus, it is clear that spiritual formation is not something new in the history of Christ's people. The ancient Christian communions of East and West show that practices of spiritual formation are as ancient as they themselves are; the very language of spiritual formation is of long-standing usage throughout many subdivisions of the Catholic church continuing today. In more ancient times Christians spoke of the *institutions* of the spiritual life[1] Moreover, the reality, if not the language, is substantially present in the Protestant wing of the church in its Reformed and Puritan forms, as well as among Anabaptists, Methodists, and many later subdivisions.

And yet, with reference to the late-twentieth-century Protestant churches in America and the West, spiritual formation clearly is something new. We are at a crucial point in the progress of Christian faith in our times, and a door of opportunity is currently open that must not be missed.

The overshadowing event of the past two centuries of Christian life has been the struggle between orthodoxy and modernism. In this struggle the primary issue has, as a matter of fact, *not* been discipleship to Christ and a transformation of soul that expresses itself in pervasive, routine obedience to his "all that I have commanded you." Instead, both sides of the controversy have focused almost entirely upon what is to be explicitly asserted or rejected as essential Christian doctrine. In the process of battles over views of Christ the Savior, *Christ the Teacher was lost on all sides.*

Discipleship as an essential issue disappeared from the churches, and with it there also disappeared realistic plans and programs for the transformation of the inmost self into Christ-likeness. One could now be a Christian forever without actually changing in heart and life. Right *profession*, positive or negative, was all that was required. This has now produced generations of professing Christians who, as a whole, do not differ in character, but only in ritual, from their nonprofessing neighbors; in addition, a massive population has now arisen in America who believe in God, even self-identify as spiritual, but will have nothing to do with churches—often as a matter of pride. What has in other days been called "nominal" Christianity now becomes "normal" Christianity, even among those whose tradition had prided itself in not being just nominal Christians.

What is new in the current revival of interest in spiritual formation is the widespread recognition that bypassing authentic, pervasive, and thorough transformation of the inner life of the human being is not desirable, not necessary, and may not be permissible. We are seeing that the human soul hungers for transformation, for wholeness and holiness, is sick and dying without it, and that it will seek it where it may—even if it destroys itself in the process. We are seeing that the church betrays itself and its world if it fails to make clear and accessible the path of thoroughgoing inner transformation through Christ.

What is the relationship between spiritual formation and salvation? How is grace involved with spiritual formation?

When "salvation" is spoken of today, where it is spoken of at all, what is almost always meant is entry into heaven when one dies. One is "saved" if one is now counted by God among those who will be admitted into His presence at death or some point thereafter. This usage of "salvation" and "saved" deprives the terminology of the general sense of *deliverance* that it bears in the Bible as a whole.

That loss is the result not only of the age-old obsession with forgiveness of sins and control over forgiveness as the only things that really matter, but also of the success of evangelicals in stressing, in recent centuries, the fundamental importance of forgiveness.

If, now, one adds that forgiveness is strictly a matter of what one (professes to) believe, we have the recipe for the consumerist Christianity-without-discipleship that we have inherited at the present moment.

If, however—and by no means denying the essential importance of correct belief and the forgiveness of sins—we understand "saving faith" to be *confidence in Jesus Christ,* the whole person, and not just in some part of what he did or said, we have the understanding of a salvation that delivers the disciple, the whole person, into a full life in the Kingdom of God. That includes progressive inner transformation of the believer, not as a condition of entry into heaven—salvation, in the common sense—but as a natural part of a whole that also includes new life, constant spiritual growth, and entry into heaven as a natural outcome rather than as the central focus. This deliverance will indeed "Be of sin the double cure, Save from wrath and make me pure."

Such deliverance is grace in every aspect. It is the gift of life in constant, interactive relationship with a living Lord, Savior, and Teacher. "And this is eternal life," Jesus himself said, "that they may know you, the only true God, and Jesus Christ whom you have sent" (John 17:3). "Knowledge" in the biblical understanding is interactive relationship. It is the redeeming relationship of disciple to master, in which unmerited favor is received from the earliest stages of repentance and forgiveness to the most advanced gifts of vision, character, service, and power (Acts 6:8). Spiritual formation is simply the process through which we "grow in the grace [certainly not in forgiveness!] and knowledge of our Lord and Savior Jesus Christ" (2 Peter 3:18).

What relationship does spiritual formation have to spirituality and the many "spiritualities" that now abound? How, if at all, is Christian spiritual formation exclusive rather than inclusive?

In the Christian context, we are spiritual to the extent that *our lives draw their direction and strength from Jesus Christ,* living Lord, through the Holy Spirit and other agencies established by God in his Kingdom, which is itself a spiritual reality. Outside that context there are, of course, other spirits (1 Corinthians 10:20, 12:2).

Spirit is unbodily personal power. It is not a mere force or energy—not even one that lies outside the framework of the physical, as that is generally understood. It is a power that functions independently of bodily and natural forces, though it can be intimately involved with them. It takes the form of ideas, attitudes, emotions, judgments, decisions, and actions. Therefore, it is personal. The human being has a spirit, as we have noted, and is basically a spiritual being, though one that is eternally specified by its bodily history. Angels are spiritual beings—the bad as well as the good. And, above all, "God is Spirit."

To the extent that the actual life of a human being is dependent upon his or her interactions with God, that human being is a spiritual person. Spirituality is the quality of life that marks such a person. In contrast, one is carnal or fleshly to the extent that this quality of life is lacking and one is operating on merely human or natural resources. The more advanced one is in the process of spiritual formation, the greater and more pervasive will be one's spirituality.

"Spiritualities" are in good supply today. Often they involve nothing more than an external form of "doing religion" or even a mere lifestyle. But in the larger cultural context the various spiritualities all represent attempts to achieve identity and power in a world where lack of a sense of self and feelings of insignificance and powerlessness crush the human soul and spirit. They all involve explicit practices—perhaps rituals, manners of dress and appearance, or special routines of diet, exercise, or social interaction—that promise to mark one out as someone special and tap into an energy that is outside the "natural." Often they intersect with the spiritual disciplines that are used within various manifestly Christian or other traditions.

Whatever is good is good, and Jesus would be the first to say so. But, generally speaking, *all* "spiritualities" are more or less exclusive of all the rest. None admit that just anything goes. All insist that there is a right and a wrong way to go about their own version of spiritual living. And you will not find any spirituality (even those that profess the utmost inclusiveness) that does not by its beliefs and practices exclude beliefs and practices of some others—indeed, most others. It is a contemporary illusion that the Christian way is *uniquely* judgmental and exclusive or is, on the whole, more exclusive than others.

The exclusiveness of Christian spirituality and spiritual formation lies simply in the life it is and brings. Let it simply be what it is, and let all see and compare. The Christian must not be close-minded and antagonistic, but need only follow and learn from Jesus Christ fully. The aim of spiritual formation is obedience to Christ from inner conformity to Christ. Such conformity will be sharply exclusive, not because of arrogance toward other spiritualities, but because of its degree of genuine love and effectual caring for all without discrimination. Inclusiveness is a grace of life that, adequately and honestly understood, must be rooted in spiritual formation in Christ. It is not an ethical or political stance that just anyone can accept or reject at will. One must have the resources for it, and, to say the least, they are not widely available.

What is the role of spiritual disciplines in spiritual formation?

By "disciplines" we understand consciously undertaken or chosen activities that enable us to do what we cannot do by direct effort. *Spiritual* disciplines are such activities, but ones specifically relevant to growth and attainment in the spiritual life. Hence, they are major factors in spiritual formation. They are a major part of what we can do to contribute to our own spiritual formation.

For example, if I find, as most do, that I cannot by *direct* effort succeed in "blessing those who curse me" or "praying without ceasing," in putting anger aside or not indulging the covetous or lustful eye, then *it is my responsibility to find out how I can train myself* (always under grace and divine guidance, we must never forget) so that I will be able to do what I cannot do just by trying in the moment of need.

"Stay awake and pray that you may not come into the time of trial" was the good advice given by Jesus to his weary friends to assist their truly willing spirits against the weakness of their natural abilities ("flesh") (Matthew 26:41). And the ancient charge was, "This book of the law shall not depart out of your mouth; you shall meditate on it day and night, so that you may be careful to act in accordance with all that is written in it. For then you shall make your way prosperous, and then you shall be successful" (Joshua 1:8). Such verses incorporate the wisdom of scripture, that we are to *take measures* to receive the spiritual assistance that we need, and that such assistance will not, in general, be passively imposed upon us or infused into us.

Solitude and silence, fasting and frugality, study and worship, service and submission—and other practices that serve in the same way (there is no complete list)—are therefore integral parts of any reliable program of spiritual formation. They should be a substantial part of our private lives and of our associations with others in the body of Christ. They do not earn merit, but they do allow us to receive from God what will not be passively bestowed. They are not righteousness but wisdom.

How are the gifts and fruit of the Spirit involved with spiritual formation?

"The fruit of the Spirit is love, joy, peace, patience, kindness, generosity, faithfulness, gentleness, and self-control" (Galatians 5:22–23). This is the same or closely associated with what Paul elsewhere calls the "fruit of light," which consists "in all that is good and right and true" (Ephesians 5:9). Obviously it is the same as love, in the *comprehensive sense* spelled out by Paul in 1 Corinthians 13 and Colossians 3:14, and which Jesus made the constant theme of his teaching.

The *fruit* of the Spirit simply is the inner character of Jesus himself that is brought about in us through the process of Christian spiritual formation. It is the *outcome* of spiritual formation. It is "Christ formed in us." It is called "fruit" because, like the fruit of trees or vines, it is an outgrowth of what we have become, not the result of a special effort to bear fruit. And we have become "fruitful" in this way because we have received the presence of Christ's Spirit through the process of spiritual formation, and now that Spirit, interacting with us, fills us with love, joy, peace. . . .

Clearly, as the fruit of the Spirit increases within us it becomes a dynamic element in its own right, in the ongoing process of spiritual formation. To be possessed of love, joy, peace . . . is to have rich resources for sustaining and enhancing a faith-full life and for growth in all dimensions of inward and outward grace. The fruit of the spirit and spiritual formation become mutually supportive as spiritual formation progresses in the individual.

The same is true, in a different way, of spiritual formation and the *gifts* of the Spirit. The gifts of the Spirit are specific supernatural abilities that are distributed among those who make up the earthly body of Christ in order that every member can benefit from all of those gifts as needed. "There are varieties of activities, but it is the same God who activates all of them in everyone. To each is given the manifestation of the Spirit for the common good" (1 Corinthians 12:6–7). Spiritual formation simply cannot go forward as it is intended by God unless the individual is incorporated in a body of believers where he or she can receive the benefit of the gifts that others have. Without the gifts, the fruit will not be produced and sustained.

Conversely, the gifts of the Spirit can only be rightly used if the one who receives and serves others by means of them is well formed in inner Christ-likeness. We are not passive in receiving and serving in the gifts of the Spirit. They are to be actively pursued, received, and cultivated. And all of this requires ongoing transformation of the inner being. Spiritual formation lays the foundation and provides a suitable framework for the exercise of gifts of the Spirit by the individual and group, and the appropriate exercise of those gifts by the individual for the group, and within the group for the individual, is necessary if spiritual formation is to go forward as it should. Gifts by themselves do little to form the spirit and the character of those who exercise them. Most important, gifts of the Spirit are not substitutes for spiritual formation, though they must be involved in it.

Isn't spiritual formation a human project, equally well expressed in many traditions other than the Christian?

Spiritual formation is indeed a human project. It is a natural part and a requirement of the human condition. No society has ever existed without it. The human being is not an instinctual animal that naturally develops what is required for its existence. It must be taught, and primary to what is taught (and caught) are the inner conditions of life (thought, emotions, intentions, etc.) that make social existence possible and enable the individual to hope for a life that is good.

Much that is good is to be found in every great human tradition of spiritual formation, and the Christian gladly respects what is good wherever it is found. We believe that "every generous act of giving, with every perfect gift, is from above, coming down from the Father of lights" (James 1:17; see also Acts 14:15–17). If we cannot afford to be generous, we possess little.

But whether the spiritual formation of the human being is "equally well expressed in many traditions other than the Christian" is a question of fact, and not something to be answered simply by being generous, or by trying not to be judgmental or superior. In many cases—for example, ancient Greek and Roman cultures, which were deeply and intelligently concerned about the right formation of the human spirit as they understood it—the answer to this question is clearly "No." It was not for nothing that Christian life and teaching supplanted those spiritualities, as they would now be called, in the early centuries of the Christian era. They were not "bullied" out of existence by trickery or by political or physical force.

It does not seem seriously likely that contemporary spiritualities—from new age to revived paganism to secularism—can hope successfully to challenge Christian spiritual formation, at its historical best, as the premier way of fostering a life to be prized among human beings, much less one pleasing before God who examines the heart. But that is not a question that we need to close off beforehand. Every fair and intelligent comparison should be made—especially with other great world religions at *their* historical best—and the decision left to the facts of the case. This is an essential part of what it would mean to follow the apostolic mandate to "honor everyone" (1 Peter 2:17) and to "test everything; hold fast to what is good" (1 Thessalonians 5:21). The Way of Christ does not dodge or deny facts, but just the opposite: it appeals to facts and urges everyone to do the same.

What is the relationship between psychology and spiritual formation?

It is natural that we should turn to psychology to understand the soul and try to meet its needs. However it may turn, psychology cannot avoid its responsibility for the understanding of the human soul—or, if you wish, life. A major tendency within the field has been "depth psychology." "What is the other kind?" we might innocently ask. "Shallow psychology?" Psychology is called to the *depths* of the human being by the very subject matter of its inquiry.

Conversely, spiritual formation also must deal with the realities of the soul. The spiritual life of the human being, even at its most elevated and ecstatic, is a psychological reality, though it is not only that. Thus, it was both natural and proper that, when it became clear earlier in this century that Bible study, prayer, the public teaching and preaching of the Word, and religious ritual—at least as they were being practiced—were obviously not meeting the often desperate needs of professing Christians, there would emerge a "Christian psychology" movement. At the time there was no literature or research in the area, except some scattered fragments of pastoral psychology, and the majority of well-known theoreticians in the field of psychology were hostile to or dismissive of Christianity and of religion in general.

The relationship between modern psychology and religion was a troubled one in its beginning and remains so to the present time. Nevertheless, a large body of psychologists who are Christians has emerged, and they have become a vital and influential presence in clinical psychology. Unfortunately, although there are many excellent psychologists who are Christians, there has emerged no truly Christian psychology—no theoretical understanding of the human soul that does justice to all the facts of our psychical existence including the spiritual life and spiritual formation. The psychologist who is Christian is forced to patch together theoretical and practical insights from many sources, some of which are antithetical to the Christian understanding of human nature and destiny.

Methodologically, of course, psychology is itself a deeply divided field. This might seem to be a hindrance to placing psychology and spiritual formation into a fruitful relationship. But it may be that it in fact provides an opportunity to develop a genuinely adequate understanding of the human self within a framework of that spiritual life for which it is suited by nature. Such an understanding, or psychology, would then serve to illuminate and direct the process of spiritual formation.

It must be said that, at present, one of the great dangers to authentically Christian spiritual formation comes from *sole reliance* upon psychological teachings and practices that simply omit the realities of Christian spiritual formation, or else substitute for them processes that do not do justice to life in the Kingdom of God. The transformation of the inner self into Christ-likeness cannot be achieved by anything other than the life of God in the soul, and anything short of this, however good and proper it may be in its place, will not be enough to meet the deepest needs of the human heart or satisfy the mind and the emotions. It will leave life adrift.

Does Christian spiritual formation really matter? Can't we get along quite well without it?

The response to this question must be, first of all, that we are not getting along quite well without it. We are, largely, without it, to be sure, but we are not doing well. The "life of quiet desperation" that most people have always lived, according to Henry David Thoreau, is at present becoming noticeably more desperate and less quiet. The sad litany of misdeeds and depraved characters that Paul listed in such places as Romans 1 and 3, Galatians 5:19–21, and 2 Timothy 3:2–7 is as up-to-date as the latest edition of the newspapers and weekly magazines or the evening news.

Education, government, business, the professions, art and entertainment, as well as the private lives of multitudes of people, stagger under the burdens of human wickedness and failure caused by others and brought on by ourselves. All of this is so common and pervasive that the normal person is almost blind to it, accepting it as "just the way things are." The processes of formation of spirit that dominate the contemporary world are a disaster when viewed in terms of their outcome: a running sore, an unhealing wound (Isaiah 1:2–9).

In addition, those who know something of the goodness and beauty of Jesus yearn to be like him or at least feel a responsibility to be like him. But they are left helpless unless they can find a path of inward transformation. Who can show them the way if the people identified with the cause of Christ in this world are not prepared to teach and exemplify a process of spiritual formation that will result in an outflow of Christ from their deepest heart and character, from their very identity, from who they are?

And from the viewpoint of those responsible to lead in Christ's program of making students from all ethnic groupings, immersing them in the reality of the triune name and teaching them to do all things he has commanded us (Matthew 28:19–20), Christian spiritual formation is simply indispensable. The lack of an understanding and implementation of it is why there is in general so little real difference between professing Christian and non-Christian today. Where can one find today any group of Christians with an actual plan to teach the people of their group to do everything Jesus said? Indeed, who is sure of the possibility of such a plan? It makes a huge difference whether spiritual formation in Christ-likeness is available to the church and to the world.

As Christian people, we stand today in a moment of great opportunity. As Paul wrote to the Corinthians, "a wide door for effective work has opened to me, and there are many adversaries" (1 Corinthians 16:9). Many blind alleys beckon, and there is much misinformation about, as well as deep antagonisms to, the way Christ calls us to go. It is important that we not see in the current interest in spiritual formation merely an invitation to keep doing what we have been doing—except now to "really mean it." The standard advice routinely given to ordinary Christians, and even to the more enthusiastic among us, is hopelessly inadequate to the needs of the heart, soul, and body. Now we must find ways that, in our current context, can succeed in honestly and thoroughly renovating the inner person so that it bears the identical vision, feelings, and character of Jesus Christ. "Go ye therefore. . . ."

CHAPTER 11

Personal Soul Care

For Ministers . . . And Others

Keep your heart with all vigilance,
For from it flow the springs of life.

—Proverbs 4:23

THE CALL OF GOD to minister the gospel is both a high honor and a noble challenge. It carries with it unique opportunities as well as special burdens and dangers for members of the clergy as well as their families. These burdens can be fruitfully borne and the dangers triumphantly overcome. But that will not happen unless the minister's "inner person" (2 Corinthians 4:16) is constantly renewed by accessing the riches of God and His Kingdom in the inner person.

The Soul and the Great Commandment

"Soul" will be understood here in its common usage as referring to the hidden or spiritual side of the person. It thus includes an individual's thoughts and feelings, along with heart, or will, with its intents and choices. It also includes an individual's bodily life and social relations, which, in their inner meaning and nature, are just as hidden as the thoughts and feelings. This inclusive under-standing of "soul," though close to what the word means on the street, is not ultimately satisfactory for analytical purposes. But it will work well enough for our needs here.

The secret to a strong, healthy, and fruitful ministerial life lies in how we work *with* God in all of these hidden dimensions of the self. Together they make up the life of the real person. They are the inescapable sources of our outward life, and they almost totally determine what effects, for good or ill, our activities as ministers will have. Natural gifts, external circumstances, and special oppor-tunities are of little significance. The good tree, Jesus said, "bears good fruit" (Matthew 7:17). If we tend to the tree, the fruit will take care of itself.

The inner dimensions of life are what are referred to in the Great Commandment: "Love the Lord your God with all your heart, and with all your soul, and with all your strength, and with all your mind; and your neighbor as yourself" (Luke 10:27). This commandment does not tell us what we must do so much as what we must cultivate in the care of our souls. This is true for all be-lievers and is certainly true for ministers of the gospel.[1] Our high calling and sacrificial service can find adequate support only in a personality totally saturated with God's kind of love, agape (see 1 Corinthians 13).

But we must be very clear that the great biblical passages on love—those already cited and others, including 1 John 4—do *not* tell us *to act as if* we loved God with our whole beings, and our neighbors as ourselves. Such an attempt, without the love of God indwelling us, would be an impossible burden. We would become angry and hopeless—as, in fact, happens to many ministers and their families, *trying to be "nice."*

Character and the "Fruit of the Spirit"

The "sudden" failures that appear in the lives of some ministers and others are never really sudden but are the surfacing of long-standing deficiencies in the "hidden person of the heart" (1 Peter 3:4). Divine love permeating every part of our lives is, in contrast, a resource adequate to every condition of life and death, as 1 Corinthians 13 assures us. This love is, in the words of Jesus, "a spring of water gushing up to eternal life" (John 4:14). And *from* those possessed of divine love there truly flow "rivers of living water" to a thirsty world (John 7:38).

The people to whom we minister and speak will not recall 99 percent of what we say to them. But they will never forget the kind of persons we are. This is certainly true of influential ministers in my own past. The quality of our souls will indelibly touch others for good or for ill. So we must never forget that the most important thing happening at any moment, in the midst of all our ministerial duties, is the kind of persons we are becoming.

God is greatly concerned with the quality of character we are building. The future He has planned for us will be built on the strength of character we forge by His grace. Intelligent, loving devotion to Christ will grow in importance through eternity and will never become obsolete.

It is God's intention that our lives should be a seamless manifestation of the fruit of the Spirit: "love, joy, peace, patience, kindness, generosity, faithfulness, gentleness, and self-control" (Galatians 5:22–23). He has made abundant provision for His indwelling our lives in the here and now. Appropriate attention to the care of our souls through His empowerment will yield this rich spiritual fruit and deliver us from the sad list of "deeds of the flesh" (Galatians 5:19–21). We can be channels of the grace of the risen Christ, and through our ministerial activities—speaking, praying, healing, administering—He can minister to others. But we must attend to the means of His grace in practical and specific ways to experience His life into and through our lives.

Practicing the Presence of God

The first and most basic thing we can and must do is to keep God before our minds. David knew this secret and wrote, "I keep the Lord always before me; because He is at my right hand, I shall not be moved. Therefore my heart is glad, and my soul rejoices; my body also rests secure" (Psalm 16:8–9).

This is *the* fundamental secret of caring for our souls. Our part in thus practicing the presence of God is to direct and redirect our minds constantly to Him. In the early time of our practicing, we may well be challenged by our burdensome habits of dwelling on things less than God. But these are habits—not the law of gravity—and can be broken. A new, grace-filled habit will replace the former ones as we take intentional steps toward keeping God before us. Soon our minds will return to God as the needle of a compass constantly returns to the north, no matter how the compass is moved. If God is the great longing of our souls, He will become the polestar of our inward beings.[2]

Jesus Christ is, of course, the Door, the Light, and the Way. We are privileged to walk in this profound reality, not just preach it. We first receive God into our minds by receiving Jesus. We open our consciousness to him and direct our attention toward him. This and nothing else is our "business as usual." The way forward then lies in intentionally keeping the scenes and words of the New Testament gospels before our minds, carefully reading and rereading them day by day. We memorize them. We revive them in word and imagination as we arise in the morning, move through the events of the day, and lie down at night. By this means we walk with Him moment by moment—the One who promised to be "with us always."

As a beginning step in this practicing process, we can choose to practice constantly returning our minds to God in Christ on a given day. Just decide to do it, and then do the best you can without harassing yourself. In the evening, then, we can review how we did, and think of ways to do it better the next day. As we continue this practice, gently but persistently, we soon will find that the person of Jesus and his beautiful words are automatically occupying our minds, instead of the clutter and noise of the world—even the church-world.

Our concentration on Jesus will be strengthened by memorization of great passages (*not* just verses) from scripture. Passages such as Matthew 5–7, John 14–17, 1 Corinthians 13, and Colossians 3 are terrific soul-growing selections. This practice of memorizing the scriptures is more important than a daily quiet time, for as we fill our minds with these great passages and have them available for our meditation, quiet time takes over the entirety of our lives. "Those of steadfast mind you keep in peace—in peace because they trust in you" (Isaiah 26:3).

God's word to Joshua, as he undertook the great task before him, was, "This book of the law shall not depart out of your mouth; you shall meditate on it day and night, so that you may be careful to act in accordance with all that is written in it. For then you shall make your way prosperous, and then you shall be successful" (Joshua 1:8). Psalm 1 demonstrates that this became a part of the recognized practice of spiritual living among the Israelites.

Meditation on Him and His Word must become an integral part of our lives too.

But how does the law get *in your mouth?* By memorization, of course. The law becomes an essential part of how we think about everything else as we *dwell on it.* Then the things that come before us during the day come in the presence of God's illuminating Word. Light dwells within us and enables us to see the things of life in the right way. "In your light we see light" (Psalm 36:9). This is the true education for ministry, and for life.

Love and Worship

As the Living Word and the written Word occupy our minds we naturally—and supernaturally—come to love God more and more because we see, clearly and constantly, how lovely He is. The glorious being of God is not just a truth we had better believe. It is an inexhaustible wonder and a delight.

The wise old Puritan Thomas Watson wrote,

> *The first fruit of love is the musing of the mind upon God. He who is in love, his thoughts are ever upon the object. He who loves God is ravished and transported with the contemplation of God. "When I awake, I am still with thee" (Psalm 139:18). The thoughts are as travelers in the mind. David's thoughts kept heaven-road. "I am still with Thee." God is the treasure, and where the treasure is, there is the heart. By this we may test our love to God. What are our thoughts most upon? Can we say we are ravished with delight when we think on God? Have our thoughts got wings? Are they fled aloft? Do we contemplate Christ and glory? . . . A sinner crowds God out of his thoughts. He never thinks of God, unless with horror, as the prisoner thinks of the judge.[3]*

In this way we enter a life, not just *times,* of worship. The hymn of heaven will be a constant presence in our inner lives: "To the one seated on the throne and to the Lamb be blessing and honor and glory and might forever and ever" (Revelation 5:13).

Worship will become the constant undertone of our lives. It is the single most powerful force in completing and sustaining restoration of our whole beings to God. Nothing can inform, guide, and sustain pervasive and radiant goodness in a person other than the true vision of God and the worship that spontaneously arises from it. Then the power of the indwelling Christ flows from us to others.

Remember, however, that we are not *trying* to worship. Worship is not another job we have to do. It is one aspect of the gift of "living water" that springs "up to eternal life" (John 7:38; 4:14). Our part is to turn our minds toward God and to attend to His graceful actions in our souls. This is the primary "care of the soul" we must exercise. Then love and worship, worship and love, flow in our lives as we walk constantly with God. By stepping with Him—in the flow of His grace—we live with spontaneity, love our neighbors, and minister the word and power of the gospel.

Opening to the Fullness of Joy

Personal soul care also requires attending to our feelings. Emotions are a real component of life and of our lives in Christ. Some ministers, and many, many people, allow their emotions to defeat them.

We do well to note, however, that *love* is the foundation of the spiritual life and *joy* is a key component in the Christ life. Joy is not pleasure, a mere sensation, but a pervasive and constant sense of well-being. Hope in the goodness of God is joy's indispensable support.

In a moment of worship and praise, Paul spontaneously expressed a benediction on the Christians in Rome: "May the God of hope fill you with all joy and peace in believing, so that you may abound in hope by the power of the Holy Spirit" (Romans 15:13). This verse addresses the profound needs of the emotional side of the Christian's life.

The great central terms of life in Christ are "faith," "hope," "love," and "peace." These are not *just* feelings; in substance, they are not feelings. They are conditions involving every part of an individual's life, including the body and the social context. They serve to equip us for the engagements of life. They do, however, have feelings that accompany them, and these positive feelings abundantly characterize those living in the presence of God. These feelings displace the bitter and angry feelings that characterize life "in the flesh"—life in human energies only. They even transform the sickening emotional tones that permeate and largely govern the world around us—even, many times, the church-world itself.

Jesus taught us to abide in God's love, "so that my joy may be in you, and that your joy may be complete" (John 15: 10–11). Our joy is complete when there is no room for more. Abiding in God's love provides the unshakable source of joy, which is in turn the source of peace. All is based in the reality of God's grace and goodness. *Faith, hope, love, joy,* and *peace*—the "magnificent five"—are inseparable from one another and reciprocally support each other. Try to imagine any one without the others!

Solitude and Silence

Among the practices that can help us attend to soul care at a basic level are *solitude* and *silence*. We practice these by finding ways to be alone and away from talk and noise. We rest, we observe, we "smell the roses"—dare we say it?—we do *nothing*. This discipline can be used of God as a means of grace. In it we may even find another reminder of grace—that we are saved, justified by His redeeming power, not by our strivings and achievements.

In drawing aside for lengthy periods of time, we seek to rid ourselves of the corrosion of soul that accrues from constant interaction with others and the world around us. In this place of quiet communion, we discover again that we *do* have souls, that we indeed have inner beings to be nurtured. Then we begin to experience again the presence of God in the inner sanctuary, speaking to and interacting with us. We understand anew that God will not compete for our attention. We must arrange time for our communion with Him as we draw aside in solitude and silence.

The Psalmist said, "Cease striving and know that I am God" (Psalm 46:10). And immediately following this, the writer affirms the success of God's mission on earth: "'I am exalted among the nations, I am exalted in the earth.' The Lord of hosts is with us; the God of Jacob is our refuge" (Psalm 46:10–11).

Other translations of this verse read, "Be still, and know that I am God" (New International Version) and "Step out of the traffic! Take a long, loving look at me" (The Message Bible). God's provision for us and for His work through us is adequate. We do not have to "make it happen." We must stop shouldering the burdens of "outcomes." These are safely in His hands.

Someone has insightfully said, "The greatest threat to devotion to Christ is service for Christ."

What a paradox! This is so easily a challenge for many ministers. Allowing service for Christ to steal our devotion to him is a radical failure in personal soul care. But it is one from which the practice of communing with Christ in times of solitude and silence can deliver us.

Time Is *Made*, Not Found

A response to giving attention to personal soul care often is "I don't have time for extensive solitude and silence. I have too much to do." The truth is that we don't have time *not* to practice solitude and silence. No time is more profitably spent than that used to heighten the quality of an intimate walk with God. If we think otherwise, we have been badly educated. The real question is, will we take time to do what is necessary for an abundant life and an abundant ministry, or will we try to get by without it?

So a couple of words of counsel are appropriate for our attending to the inner life. First, God never gives anyone too much to do. We do that to ourselves or allow others to do it to us. We may be showing our lack of confidence in God's power and goodness, though possibly our models and our education have failed us. Second, the exercise of God's power in ministry never, by itself, amends character, and it rarely makes up for our own foolishness. God's power can be actively and wisely sought and received by us only as we seek to grow by grace into Christ-likeness. Power *with* Christ-like character is God's unbeatable combination of triumphant life in the Kingdom of God on earth and forever. Power without Christ's character gives us our modern-day Sampsons and Sauls.

Knowing Christ through times spent away in solitude and silence will let our "joy be complete" (John 16:24). It will bring over us a pervasive sense of well-being, no matter what is happening around us. Hurry and the loneliness of leadership will be eliminated. We can allow the peace of God to sink deeply into our lives and extend through our relationships to others (see Matthew 10:12–13).

A young Christian who had been guided into the effective practice of solitude and silence had this to say:

The more I practice this discipline, the more I appreciate the strength of silence. The less I become skeptical and judgmental, the more I learn to accept the things I didn't like about others, and the more I accept them as uniquely created in the image of God. The less I talk, the fuller are words spoken at an appropriate time. The more I value others, the more I serve them in small ways, and the more I enjoy and celebrate my life. The more I celebrate, the more I realize that God has been giving me wonderful things in my life, and the less I worry about my future. I will accept and enjoy what God is continuously giving to me. I think I am beginning to really enjoy God.[4]

Experiencing God through the practice of connecting with Him via this discipline brings rich rewards.

Planning for Fullness of Life

Our discussion so far has been more illustrative than expository. Solitude and silence are absolutely basic in our responsibility to soul care. But they also open before us the whole area of *disciplines* for the spiritual life. It is vital for us to keep before us that there are tried and true ways we can pursue abundant life in Christ. These ways are often referred to as "spiritual disciplines."[5] We can and must incorporate these into our lives as completely reliable ways of personal soul care. There is no substitute for this.

A person could make a long list of such disciplines, drawing on the history of Christ's people. The list would certainly include fasting, which when rightly practiced has incredible power for the transformation of character and for ministry. On this list would also be such practices as frugality, service, celebration, prayer (as a discipline), journaling, fellowship, accountability relationships, submission, confession, and many others.

There is no such thing as a complete list of the disciplines. Any activity that is in our power and enables us to achieve by grace what we cannot achieve by direct effort is a discipline of the spiritual life.[6]

As we seek to know Christ by incorporating appropriate disciplines into our lives, we must keep in mind that they are not ways of earning merit. They also are not paths of suffering or self-torment. They are not heroic. They are not righteousness. But they are indispensable wisdom.

Once we learn that grace is not opposed to effort (action)—though it is opposed to earning (attitude)—the way is open for us to "work out" all that is involved in our salvation, not only "with fear and trembling" but also with the calm assurance that it is God who is at work in us to accomplish all of His goodwill (see Philippians 2:12–13).

When we have settled into a life of sensible disciplines with our ever-present Teacher, then Peter's admonition (2 Peter 1:5–7) to add virtue to our faith, knowledge or understanding to our virtue, self-control to our knowledge, patience to our self-control, godliness to our patience, brotherly kindness to our godliness, and divine love (agape) to our brotherly kindness will prove to be a sensible plan for life. God will use this course of action to help others through our ministries as well.

"For if you do this," Peter continues (verse 10), "you will never stumble." In our walk with God in Christ there will be provided to us, from "his riches in glory" (Philippians 4:19), sweetness and strength of character, profundity of insight and understanding, and abundance of power to manifest the glory of God in life and in ministry—no matter the circumstances! And "entry into the eternal kingdom of our Lord and Savior Jesus Christ will be richly provided for you" (2 Peter 1:11)—long before you die.

Further Reading

Thomas à Kempis. *The Imitation of Christ*. Many editions available. Apart from the Bible itself, this is undoubtedly the most republished work in Christian history. Absolutely indispensable.

Baxter, Richard. *The Practical Works of Richard Baxter* (Baker Book House, 1981).

Bouyer, Louis. *A History of Christian Spirituality*. 3 vols. (Seabury Press, 1982).

De Sales, Francis. *Introduction to the Devout Life*. (Doubleday, 1957).

Finney, Charles. *Revival Lectures* (Fleming H. Revell Co., n.d.).

Law, William. *A Serious Call to a Devout and Holy Life* (Paulist Press, 1978). Many editions available.

Murray, Andrew. Especially *Humility* and *Absolute Surrender*. Many editions.

Nouwen, Henri. *The Way of the Heart* (Ballantine Books, 1981).

DISCIPLESHIP
OF THE SOUL
AND THE MIND

CHAPTER 12

Spiritual Disciplines, Spiritual Formation, and the Restoration of the Soul

The law of the Lord is perfect, restoring the soul.

—Psalm 19:7

He restores my soul. He guides me in the paths of righteousness for His name's sake.

—Psalm 23:3

A Renewed Interest in Spirituality

Currently there is much interest in spiritual disciplines and the process of spiritual formation. This derives from a sense of our urgent need for mental and emotional health, as well as spiritual depth, and from the simultaneous realization that recent standard practice of American Christianity is not meeting that need.[1] Many serious and thoughtful Christians are looking for ways into an intelligent and powerful Christ-likeness that can inform their entire existence and not just produce special religious moments. Practices and concepts that have had a long life in the Christian past are being experienced and explored anew, and many involved in the field of psychology are taking a professional interest in them and in the soul.[2]

This is a very hopeful development. But unless the interest in spirituality, as it is now sometimes called, finds a foundation in the nature of human personality and in God's redemptive interactions therewith, it will be at most a passing fad. Moreover, it is possible for people not only to be disappointed in this area, but seriously harmed. We need to think deeply and clearly about spiritual disciplines and spiritual formation, and in particular about their relationships with the human soul, the deepest dimension of human personality.

Assumptions for This Discussion

In what follows I shall not deal with the specifically philosophical questions about the soul, though I shall have to touch upon a number of them. Fortunately, Dr. J. P. Moreland's essay, "Restoring the Substance to the Soul of Psychology," in this issue of the *Journal of Psychology and Theology* gives an excellent treatment of the philosophical issues, and I suggest a thorough reading of that paper as a preliminary to what follows.

As he carefully explains, the human soul must be treated as an entity in its own right, with its own peculiar nature and relationships. It is the fundamental but not the only component of a human person and life. That is the position uniformly maintained by the Western tradition of thought up to Hume, and in many quarters long thereafter.[3] The soul is, as Professor Moreland indicates, a substance, in the sense that it is an individual entity that has properties and dispositions natural to it, endures through time and change, and receives and exercises causal influence on other things, most notably the *person* of which it is the most fundamental part.

The soul is not a simple or noncomplex being, except in the sense of not having *spatial* parts. This in fact confuses many people, who when they think "part" can only think spatial part. Of course, anything with spatial parts could, precisely, not be a soul. One is likely to forget that there are many other things with no spatial parts, such as a chord played in music or the flavors in a soup. Concepts like part, property, complexity, and so on, have to be handled with extreme care when one comes to deal with persons. Professor Moreland does this in an exemplary fashion.

Now, a soul is essentially a component of a person—as is the mind and will, which are among the person's essential parts—and does not exist without a person whose soul it is. It or its parts cannot lie around like a spare part of an automobile or computer. But it is equally true that persons do not exist without a soul. A *person* is a living entity that has a certain kind of life: primarily one of self-determination in terms of adopted values, with the possibility (and vital need) of worship. The soul is that entity within a person that integrates all of the components of his or her life into *their* life, *one* life.

The soul is not a *physical* entity, of course, and efforts to think of it in such terms underlie most of the "modern" objections to the soul in intellectual contexts. Consequently, knowledge of it cannot be achieved on the basis of sense perception or physical theory. But that is no objection against it. For sense perception gives us knowledge of very little of significant human interest, least of all knowledge of knowledge itself.

Empiricism (later often called "positivism") is simply a failed ideological gambit in Western culture that prevailed from roughly the eighteenth century on and should be regarded as nothing more than an instructive, if somewhat unfortunate, historical episode. It arbitrarily specifies the senses or feeling as boundary markers for knowledge and reality. But it cannot guide us in the interpretation of knowledge and reality, for it fundamentally misconstrues them. Its primary function was to replace religious orthodoxy with a secular, epistemological orthodoxy, as cultural authority was passing from religious to merely intellectual institutions in modern Western society. As an orthodoxy, it is, of course, repressive and, among other things, makes impossible knowledge of the human self. One can judge for oneself the cost of this by candidly observing the intellectual and moral chaos that rules modern society—not least, intellectual society itself. Of course, empiricism is not itself an empirical theory, and in the nature of the case could never be. It stands self-refuted.

So in what follows I shall presuppose (pointing to Professor Moreland for details of argument) a "classical" view of the soul and the person, along the above lines. People in our intellectual culture today vaguely suppose, by and large, that "something has been found out" that proves this view wrong. Adopting postures and phraseologies of thinkers such as Hume and Nietzsche, they often heap scorn on Plato, Descartes, and dualism. *But nothing has been found out to that effect.* Apart from the unfortunate, though historically necessary, episode of empiricism/positivism/naturalism and its paralyzing aftereffects, one would never have supposed it had.

I shall also presuppose in what follows that biblical revelation is a source of knowledge. We have *knowledge* of a subject matter when *we are able to represent it as it in fact is, on an appropriate basis of thought and experience.* Authority is one source of knowledge provided that it is good authority. Most of what we know we know on the basis of one authority or another—much of it from reading books or listening to outstanding scientists and thinkers. Of course, any authority should be open to any fair and reasonable question, and we should always evaluate authorities in whatever appropriate ways are possible. Similarly for the Bible. And when it is properly used, it is a source of knowledge about the most important things in human life: the nature of the human being and its relationship to God.

Descriptive Distinctions Within the Human Being

Now, any thoughtful treatment of the human being will eventuate in a list of our natural capacities and their interactions. You see this over and over in the works of philosophers and psychologists and even literary people, East and West. The list necessarily includes our capacities to represent or think, to feel (sensate and emotional), and to choose or will. In addition, there are the bodily and social dimensions of the human self. These last are of fundamental importance to incarnate personal beings such as we. Human life, *human* capacities, are inseparable from them.

But these capacities and dimensions of the human being are all interactively related to one another in that they are the capacities and dimensions of a single person. It is my thought of a disaster that evokes my fear and causes my palms to sweat. It is my perception of brake lights ahead that leads me to put on my brakes. It is my anger or my lust that sways me toward doing what I know to be wrong, and my reverence for persons or for God that enables me to treat others with compassion and truthfulness, and so forth.

Moreover, acts and states *within* the range of each of these distinctive capacities are essentially interrelated. My anger affects my other feelings, and conversely. The representations and judgments in my train of thought affect each other. My selection of inclusive goals affects my particular choices, and conversely. Out of the rich texture of interrelationships within and between the various capacities and dimensions of the human being there arises the individual human personality and its life.

This much, I think, we must take as simple description. It is hard to imagine a theory that would seriously deny any of it. But we have to go beyond description to make sense of what it brings to light, and it is in so doing that conceptualization and theory have their proper place.

Soul as Source and Coordinating Principle of Life

The most illuminating and rational way of thinking about the soul is to regard it as that component of the total person that coordinates all of the capacities and dimensions of the human being and leads to their interactive development to form an individual life.

Modern thinkers from Hume to Derrick Parfit, driven by empiricism or at least antisubstantialism, have tried to avoid this uniquely coordinative source within the human being by taking the descriptive elements of life as atoms and reconstructing the whole person in terms of various relationships between those atoms. It seems clear that this attempt fails, as Hume himself acknowledges for his own attempt. Rather than "reconstructing" the person, the person is simply lost. The loss of the self is the central reality of nineteenth- and twentieth-century thought in all its dimensions. This is something upon which, I suppose, most informed people will agree.

The Classical View

In contrast, the route taken both by the most influential Greek thinkers, Plato and Aristotle among them, and by the biblical writers is to take the soul as an entity in its own right. The soul is thought of by them as the *source* of life within the individual, and simultaneously as its ordering principle.

Thus, Plato presents the soul as a self-moved mover.[4] The element of spontaneity that characterizes living things over against nonliving things (stones, chairs) was attributed to the possession of soul, and the differences in kind between living things (plant, animal, human, divine) to possession of souls of different *kinds*. That is, souls that originate different types of spontaneous activities (growth, nutrition, reproduction, sensation, emotion, thought, will) and that arrange and order those activities in diverse ways conducive to the well-being of the living thing in question are souls that differ in nature. The differing activities and life flow form the difference in inner character.

Although soul is a cosmic principle for both Plato and Aristotle, their overwhelming concern is to understand the *human* soul. They know all too well that things often go badly in human life, and they understand this to be, precisely, the result of a misfunction of the inner source of life. It is an expression of *disorder* in the soul itself. Specifically, for them, it is a failure of reason (the capacity to think and understand) to supervise appropriately human emotion and appetites, including bodily feelings. Such failure of supervision occurs, as they well understood, on both the individual and the social levels.

The solution to the problem of a proper ordering of the soul lay, for Plato, in providing a proper education for those who would lead society in various capacities, especially in the area of legislation. Aristotle differed very little from him on this point. On his view, the legislator must carefully study the human soul, because he legislates entirely with a view to producing good human souls.[5] If society is rightly organized by legislation, his presumption was, all will go well both in the individual and in society. If the inner source and ordering principle is functioning rightly, the life that flows from it can only be as it should be.

The Biblical Picture

One sees here the same assumption about human existence as is found in the biblical sources. "Keep your heart"—the source and center of life—"with all vigilance," the Proverbalist says, "for out of it comes your life" (Proverbs 4:23). But of course, the ultimate point of reference in the biblical context is not human education and legislation, but divine. "My child, be attentive to my words; incline your ear to my sayings. Do not let them escape from your sight; keep them within your heart. For they are life to those who find them, and healing to all their flesh" (Proverbs 4:20–22).

The same basic idea is expressed in Jesus's teachings that a good tree cannot bring forth bad fruit, and that what defiles the human being comes only from the heart (Mark 7:15–23). In the biblical teachings, of course, the force of revelation is added to the human insight that the *source* is within, in the deep levels of personality, and that the order or disorder of life as a whole is to be traced to order and disorder at that deeper level.

A Useful Analogy

One can compare the soul to the computer at the center of a computerized production system of some sort, say an automobile factory or a print shop. More crudely still, it is like the timing mechanism on an automatic appliance such as a dishwasher. The computer or timer is a distinct entity in its own right. It has an inherent nature (parts, properties) that allows it to coordinate the various activities and states in the system as a whole. Its own ability to function depends upon it being appropriately positioned in the larger whole.

Of course, the computer or timer is a strictly physical entity, whereas the soul is not. But then, the whole that it runs is also a physical entity, as the person is not—even though the human person has essential physical components in his or her life. Granting significant dissimilarities, it is helpful to think of the soul as the "computer" that operates all dimensions of the human system by governing and coordinating what goes on in them. It has its own nature, parts, properties, and internal and external relations, as indicated earlier.

The Soul Distanced from the Person

It is this sense of a deeper level of the self that accounts for characteristic "soul" language found in the Bible and elsewhere. For example, the soul is typically *addressed,* or it may be referred to in the third person, by the very person whose soul it is. It is treated as if it had, in some measure, a life of its own. And in fact it does. Thus: "Why are you cast down, O my soul . . . hope in God" (Psalm 42:5); "bless the Lord, O my soul" (Psalm 103:1); "my soul keeps your decrees" (Psalm 119:167); "my soul magnifies the Lord" (Luke 1:47).

One reason why the book of Psalms so powerfully affects us is that it is a soul book. It is the premier soul book on earth. It touches us at the deepest levels of our lives, far beyond our conscious thoughts and endeavors. It expresses and helps us to express the most profound parts of our lives. This element of depth and distance is a primary characterization of soul. It is of the very nature of the soul. Thus, Thomas Moore, in his *Care of the Soul,* offers nothing more, in the way of a concept of *soul,* than that it is the "deep" part of the self.

Now, just because the soul is the source and unity of our life, it is sometimes used as equivalent with the person. This is common biblical usage as well as an ordinary way of speaking. "Poor soul," we say when we mean "poor person." And one does not respond to the international signal of extreme distress, "SOS" ("Save Our Souls"), by trying to save anything other than the persons involved. Along with the soul, the person is, of course, saved. When the Psalmist says, "My soul is among the lions" (57:4), he means *he* is among the lions. And when the writer of Hebrews speaks of the "saving of the soul" (10:39), he means the saving of the person. With the soul, everything else comes along. But still, the person is not identical with his soul. There is much to the person other than the soul, and in this lies hope for the restructuring of the broken and corrupted soul.

Sin as Psychological Reality

The condition of normal human life is one where the inner resources of the person are weakened or dead, and where the factors of human life do not interrelate as they were intended by their nature and function to do. This is sin in the singular: not an act but a condition. It is not that we are wrong, but that our inner components are no longer hooked up correctly. The wires are crossed, as it were. We are *wrung*, twisted. Our thinking, our feeling, our very bodily dispositions are defective and connected wrongly with reference to life as a whole.

All of this comes to a head in the will (the same as the heart, or the human spirit). The will stands, so to speak, in the shambles of the human system, flailing about in ineffectual and sporadic jerks or driven into complete passivity.

Paul gives us definitive language for our condition before the broken and corrupted soul: We are "dead through trespasses and sins" (Ephesians 2:1). "For I do not do the good I want, but the evil I do not want is what I do" (Romans 7:19). We know the phenomenon even if we know nothing of Paul. Of course, there is some matter of degree here. But no human being entirely escapes the blight of the will, and in some it becomes a matter of total dysfunctionality and misery, no longer rebellion but sickness. The person is effectively turned away from his or her own good. The individual may and often does wish to be good and to do what is right, but he or she is *prepared,* is *set,* to do evil. It is what the individual is ready to do without thinking.

In this condition, the mind is confused, ignorant, and misguided. The emotions are simultaneously dominant of personality and in conflict with one another. The body and the social environment are filled with regular patterns of wrongdoing and are constantly inclined toward doing what is wrong. In this condition, the intellect finds reasons why what is bad is good (or at least is not bad) and what is good is bad (or at least is not good).

Paul, that deeply thoughtful man, once again has the apt description of the situation: "They know God's decree, that those who practice such things deserve to die—yet they not only do them but even applaud others who practice them" (Romans 1:32).

Always, we may be sure, with elaborate justifications! For that becomes a major function of mind in the broken state of soul. This is the deeper source of the saying from ancient Greek culture that "whom the gods would destroy they first make mad." This self-justifying, rationalizing activity is a perverted expression of the natural role of mind in the human economy. Its natural role is to find the right way to act—the way that is just and right, and that leads to what is good. When the person as a whole is committed to doing what is wrong and evil, the mind turns from reason to rationalization. From establishing what is right in order to do it, it turns to establishing that *whatever* is done is "right" and "good," or at least "necessary." That is the madness.

The "Light" of the Gospel

Hence, the traditional pattern of Christian conversion or recovery must begin with a new thought that comes from outside the entire human system. It is one that leads to new emotions and makes possible a new act of will. The new thought is, of course, the information content of the gospel. It is a new picture of the real world I actually live in. That world turns out to be made and governed by a person who loved this world and myself so much that He sent His son to save me from total ruin. I am unable to discover this on my own, especially surrounded as I am by layer upon layer of thought, feeling, and custom turned against it. And *especially* since I have through long usage internalized all this and identify *it* with real life and *my* life.

This new thought, which is the gospel, breaks through the intellectual shroud of my spiritual death by a supernatural force. That is grace in action, the approach of the graceful God. And, as it breaks through, it brings a new emotion. This new emotion is a complex one, combining longing for the new thought to be true and grief in the realization that I am set against it in the deepest reaches of my being. That is classical "conviction of sin," and with it a force begins to move within the broken soul that can lead to its restoration. But the force is not yet "owned" by the individual. Conviction of sin can be resisted, and usually is resisted for a time. During this period the individual has not yet identified with the touch of the divine hand upon his soul. The new thought and the new emotion are not yet his, but are an imposition, a foreign presence in his life that he may even resent and reject.

Yet they make *possible* a new choice that will make them his own. The will, a fundamental dimension of the human soul, can only act from ideas or representations, on the one hand, and emotions or feelings, on the other. It is a power of self-determination, to be sure, and an inherent part of a human soul. But it does not have *absolute* independence and self-direction. That is for God alone. Now, given the new thought and the new emotion, with the accompanying grace, I am capable of a new choice. I can side with the thought, I can side with the emotion. I can say, "Yes, I want this thought to be true, and the response that I feel toward God and myself on the basis of it is *my* attitude." In so doing, I choose to trust God.

The divine hand that has moved of its own initiative in the darkness of my broken soul and life is now grasped by what little strength I may have, and my grasping hand is then grasped in turn by the person whose hand I take. This is the reality of the "birth from above." Flowing back and forth across the hands clasped is the reality of a personal relationship. My mind, emotions, will, and embodied socialized self begin to feel, throughout, the presence of God's life. My broken, corrupted soul begins to reform its powers. I begin to rise toward light and wholeness.

The grand old Wesleyan hymn is amazingly deep theologically, and accurate as psychological description:

> Long my imprisoned spirit lay,
>   Fast bound by sin and nature's night,
> Thine eye dispersed a quickening ray,
>   I woke, the dungeon flamed with light.
> My chains fell off, my spirit free,
>   I rose, went forth, and followed Thee.

Becoming Active in Spiritual Growth

While the initiative in the revival and reformation of the soul originally comes from what lies beyond us, we are never *merely* passive at *any* point in the process. This is clear from the biblical *imperatives* to repent and to believe, and—for the person with new life already in them—to put off the old person and put on the new, to work out the salvation that is given to us, etc., etc. It is certainly true, as Jesus said to his friends, "apart from me you can do nothing" (John 15:5). But it is equally true for them that "If you do nothing, it will be without me." In the process of spiritual reformation under grace, passivity does not exclude activity and activity does not exclude passivity.

Hence, the invasion of the personality by life from above does not by itself form the personality in the likeness of Christ. It does not of itself restore the soul into the wholeness intended for it in its creation. It does not alone bring one to the point where "the things I would, that I *do,* and the things I would not, I *do not,*" where "sin will have no dominion over you" (Romans 6:14). Rather, I must learn and accept the responsibility of moving *with* God in the transformation of my own personality. Intelligent and steady implementation of plans for change are required if I am to lose the incoherence of the broken soul and take on the easy obedience and fulfillment of the person who lives ever more fully within the Kingdom of God and the friendship of Jesus.

Planning for Routine Progress in Wholeness

The question then is *How,* precisely, am I to go about doing my part in the process of my own transformation? What is my *plan?* The answer to this question is, in general formulation: by practice of spiritual disciplines, or disciplines for the spiritual life. We may not know or use this terminology, but what it refers to is what we must do.

What is discipline? A discipline is an activity within our power— something we can do—that brings us to a point where we can do what we at present cannot do by direct effort. Discipline is in fact a natural part of the structure of the human soul, and almost nothing of any significance in education, culture, or other attainments is achieved without it. Everything from learning a language to weight-lifting depends upon it, and its availability in the human makeup is what makes the individual human being responsible for the kind of person he or she becomes. Animals may be trained, but they are incapable of discipline in the sense that is essential to human life.

The principle of discipline is even more important in the spiritual life. Once in a seminar a wealthy and influential leader said to me that he could not help "exploding" when he tried to talk to his rebellious son. I said, "Of course you can." He looked at me in astonishment and denial. "Just tell your wife," I continued, "that the next time you blow up at him you will contribute $5,000 to her favorite charity, and also every time thereafter." He paused, and a smile of recognition tugged at the corners of his mouth.

But while this sort of case makes a point, it does not really convey the main point of discipline in the spiritual life. Spiritual disciplines are not primarily for the solving of behavioral problems, though that is one of their effects. That is why, contrary to popular opinion, the various twelve-step programs are not programs of spiritual discipline. They *are* disciplines, of course. Quite precisely, they focus on things we, for the most part, can do—attend meetings, publicly own up, call on others from the group in times of need, etc., etc.—to enable us to do what we cannot do by direct effort—stay sober. But staying sober, while desperately important for the alcoholic, is hardly a mark of spiritual attainment. The same is true of not exploding at one's son.

The aim of disciplines in the spiritual life—and, specifically, in the following of Christ—is the transformation of the total state of the soul. It is the renewal of the whole person from the inside, involving differences in thought, feeling, and character that may never be manifest in outward behavior at all. This is what Paul has in mind when he speaks of putting off the old man and putting on the new, "renewed to resemble in knowledge the one who created us . . ." (Colossians 3:10).

The genius of the moral teachings of Jesus and his first students was his insistence that you cannot keep the law by trying not to break the law. That will only make a Pharisee of you and sink you into layers of hypocrisy. Instead, you have to be transformed in the functions of the soul so that the deeds of the law are a natural outflow of who you have become. This is spiritual formation in the Christian way, and it must *always* be kept in mind when we consider Jesus's teachings about various behaviors—in the Sermon on the Mount and elsewhere.

For example, his famous teaching about turning the other cheek. If all you intend is to do *that,* you will find you can do it with a heart still full of bitterness and vengefulness. If, on the other hand, you become a person who has the interior character of Christ, remaining appropriately vulnerable will be done as a matter of course, and you will not think of it as a big deal.

An intelligent, balanced, persistent course of the standard disciplines, well known from the sweep of Christian history and written sources, can serve the individual well and is in fact essential to the development of his or her cooperative relationship with Christ. While these disciplines are by no means all that is involved—not *everything* in this process—they are indispensable. They do not take the place, and they cannot be effective without, the word of the gospel and the movements of the Spirit of God in our lives. But neither will the gospel and the Spirit take their place. Some people, of course, are unable to put them into practice. Spiritual disciplines are not "in their power," at least for the time being. Such persons need help and ministry of various kinds, depending on the particular case and circumstances. But people who are not totally shattered, and who have experienced the birth from above, can usually, with simple instruction and encouragement, begin to make real progress toward wholeness by gentle and persistent practices such as solitude and silence, fasting, scripture memorization, regular times of corporate and individual praise and worship, and so on. The various disciplines minister to different and complementary aspects of our wrungness and brokenness.[6]

Solitude and silence are primary means for correcting the distortions of our embodied social existence. Our good ideas and intentions are practically helpless in the face of what our body in the social context is poised to do automatically. Jesus, of course, understood all this very well. Thus, he knew that Peter's declarations that he would not deny him were irrelevant to what he would actually do in the moment of trial. And in fact the social setting and Peter's deeply ingrained habits moved him to deny Jesus three times, one right after the other, even though he had been warned most clearly of what was going to happen.

The wrung habits of mind, feeling, and body are keyed so closely and so routinely to the social setting that being alone and being quiet for lengthy periods of time are, for most people, the only way they can take the body and soul out of the circuits of sin and allow them to find a new habitual orientation in the Kingdom of the Heavens. Choosing to do this and learning how to do it effectively is a basic part of what we can do to enable ourselves to do what we cannot do by direct effort, even with the assistance of grace.

Indeed, solitude and silence are powerful means to grace. Bible study, prayer, and church attendance, among the most commonly prescribed activities in Christian circles, generally have little effect for soul transformation, as is obvious to any observer. If all the people doing them were transformed to health and righteousness by them, the world would be vastly changed. Their failure to bring about the change is precisely because the body and soul are so exhausted, fragmented, and conflicted that the prescribed activities cannot be appropriately engaged in and by and large degenerate into legalistic and ineffectual rituals. Lengthy solitude and silence, including *rest,* can make them very powerful.

But we must choose these disciplines. God will, generally speaking, not compete for our attention. If we will not withdraw from the things that obsess and exhaust us into solitude and silence, He will usually leave us to our own devices. He calls us to "be still and know." To the soul disciplined to wait quietly before Him, to *lavish* time upon this practice, He will make Himself known in ways that will redirect our every thought, feeling, and choice. The body itself will enter a different world of rest and strength. And the effects of solitude and silence will reverberate through the social settings where one finds oneself.

Fasting, another one of the central disciplines, retrains us away from dependence upon the satisfaction of desire and makes the Kingdom of God a vital factor in our concrete existence. It is an indispensable application of what Jesus called *the cross.* In the simplest of terms, the cross means not doing or getting what one wants. And of course, from the merely human viewpoint, getting what one wants is everything. Anger is primarily a response to frustration of will, and it makes no difference, to the broken soul, if what is willed is something perfectly trivial. What is called road rage, now epidemic and often fatal in our society, is only a case in point.

Fasting, which primarily concerns voluntary abstention from food, all or some, and can also be extended to drink, has the function of freeing us from having to have what we want. We learn to remain calm, serene, and strong when we are deprived—even severely deprived. If our desires are unsatisfied, we learn—"So, exactly, what?"

Positively, we learn that God meets our needs in His own ways. There are "words of God" other than "bread" or physical food, and these are capable of directly sustaining our bodies along with our whole being (Deuteronomy 8:3–5; Matthew 4:4; John 4:32–34). Fasting liberates us, on the basis of experience, into the abundance of God. The effects of this for the reordering of our souls are vast.

Christian practitioners through the ages have understood that to fast well brought one out from under domination of desire and feeling generally, not just in the area of food.

Scripture memorization is the final specific discipline we will mention here. It is in fact a subdivision of the discipline of study. Study as a spiritual discipline is, in general, the focusing of the mind upon God's works and words. In study our mind takes on the order in the object studied, and that order invariably forms the mind itself and thereby the soul and the life arising out of it. Thus, the law of God kept before the mind brings the order of God into our mind and soul. The soul is restored as the law becomes the routine pattern of inward life and outward action. We are integrated by it into the movements of the eternal Kingdom.

The primary freedom we have is always the choice of where we will place our minds. That freedom is enhanced by the practice of solitude, silence, and fasting. We can then effectively fill our minds with the Word of God, preserved in the scriptures. To that end, memorization is vital. It is astonishing how little of the Bible is known by heart by people who profess to honor it. If we do not know it, how can it help us? It cannot. Memorization, in contrast, enables us to keep it constantly before our minds. And that makes it possible to consciously hold ourselves within the flow of God's life that is *Torah* and *Logos*.

There is no greater disciplinary verse in the entire Bible than Joshua 1:8 (mirrored and expanded in Psalm 1 and Matthew 6:33), and none more instructive on the restoration of the soul. There we read, "This book of the law shall not depart out of your mouth; you shall meditate on it day and night, so that you may be careful to act in accordance with all that is written in it. For then you shall make your way prosperous, and then you shall be successful." Memorization enables us to mumble and meditate, which enables us to *do,* which enables us, in turn, to be successful (and He will define "successful" for us) because we are walking in God's ways with an interior character like His.

If someone says he or she cannot memorize scripture, that person probably is living in a condition to which solitude and silence and fasting are the only answer. The spiritual disciplines require one another to achieve their maximal effect. Scripture memorization, on the other hand, strengthens those other disciplines. Together the disciplines well known among Christians through the ages can fill out a reasonable and time-tested plan for our part in "work[ing] out our own salvation with fear and trembling; for it is God who is at work in you, enabling you both to will and to work for his good pleasure" (Philippians 2:12–13).

Spiritual Formation

Spiritual formation, as commonly referred to nowadays, is a matter of reforming the broken soul of man in a recovery from its alienation from God. Really, it is *soul reformation.* The spirit in man is not the soul, but is the central part of the soul, the power of self-determination. It is the heart or will: the power, embedded in the soul, of choosing. It is that in the human being that must above all be restructured. From it, then, the divine restructuring can be extended to the rest of the life, including the body. For the spirit or will also is the executive center of the self, which—given the birth from above—enables the individual to restructure or reprogram the wrung soul, along with the body, through spiritual disciplines. These disciplines, somewhat ironically, are all matters of *utilizing the body* in special ways that access grace and truth to the whole person.

It is in union with these activities that God "restores my soul." The result is that I walk in paths of righteousness on His behalf as a natural expression of my renewed inner nature. Now my experiences and responses are all hooked up correctly, or at least increasingly so. To develop a thorough understanding of this process and outcome on the basis of factual studies would be a major step toward attaining a genuinely Christian psychology or theory of the soul.

This is essential, not only to those with a Christian or even a merely psychological interest. We are now in a state of epistemic crisis in all our professions, because knowledge of the human self cannot fit the categories socially regarded as acceptable. Law and education, medicine and economics—and must we not add religion?—are working in the dark for lack of understanding of the human soul, of what makes human life what it is. To develop accurate knowledge of the human soul is the primary need of our times, and who should be in better position to provide it than the Christian psychologist? If we accept the reality of the soul, we can begin to explore its nature and to seek the means, of whatever kind, that are effective in its restoration.

Further Reading

Foster, R. *Celebration of Discipline,* 3rd ed. (HarperSanFrancisco, 1998).

Moore, T. *Care of the Soul* (HarperCollins, 1992).

Moreland, J. P. "Restoring the Substance to the Soul of Psychology." *Journal of Psychology and Theology* 26 (March 1998): 29–43.

Ventura, M. "Soul in the Raw: America Can Sell Anything, Including That Most Ephemeral Commodity: The Soul." *Psychology Today* 30, no. 3 (1997): 58–83.

Willard, D. *The Spirit of the Disciplines* (HarperSanFrancisco, 1988).

———. *The Divine Conspiracy* (HarperSanFrancisco, 1998).

———. *Renovation of the Heart* (NavPress, 2002).

CHAPTER 13

Christ-Centered Piety

The Heart of the Evangelical

M Y APPROACH to the subject of piety here rests upon the assumption that *one* of the great engines of individual and social transformation since the Reformation has been "evangelical" thought and experience. Not always under that name, perhaps, but at least as a sustaining force. My interest in evangelicalism is not, however, simply in its power as a social phenomenon, which has ebbed and flowed, but also, and mainly, in its power over individual human existence. For various reasons, a great deal of that power has currently been lost.

"Piety" refers to the inward and outward states and acts that constitute a life of devotion—chiefly to God, but commonly also to parents (as when we speak of "filial piety") and, by a further extension, to any relationship appropriately similar to that of child to parent (when we speak, for example, of a school as "alma mater"). Externally viewed, piety consists of the routine activities carried out in a sustaining relationship that honors those who give us life and well-being. It can steady us, give our lives a substance, and move us toward the highest human ideals. That is piety at its best. Can anything replace it?

In his report for the academic year 1986–87, then Harvard president Derek Bok wrote, "Religious institutions no longer seem as able as they once were to impart basic values to the young. In these circumstances, universities, including Harvard, need to think hard about what they can do in the face of what many perceive as a widespread decline in ethical standards." President Bok went on to say,

> Today's course on applied ethics does not seek to convey a set of moral truths but tries to encourage students to think carefully about complex moral issues. . . . The principal aim of the course is not to impart "right answers" but to make students more perceptive in detecting ethical problems when they arise, better acquainted with the best moral thought that has accumulated through the ages, and more equipped to reason about the ethical issues they will face in their own personal and professional lives.

At the end of the report, he concluded,

> Despite the importance of moral development to the individual student and the society, one cannot say that higher education has demonstrated a deep concern for the problem. . . . Especially in large universities, the subject is not treated as a serious responsibility worthy of sustained discussion and determined action by the faculty and administration.

I am a great admirer of Derek Bok, and I regularly use his book *The Cost of Talent* (1993) in a course I teach on "The Professions and the Public Good in American Life" at the University of Southern California. At the conclusion of that book, he notes the quandary over what to do about the unequal distribution of income among the professions, since many of the most important ones (especially teaching and public service) are "starving" on the scale of remuneration. He can only say that we need to *change our values.*

To be sure. But where do we turn to accomplish that? It is understandable that we should not pay much attention to moral development in our universities if there is *no basis in knowledge* upon which to deal with it. And bluntly put, that is where we stand today. Many intellectuals don't even think of morality as an area of knowledge. Many of the most important books written on the subject of moral values during the past eighty or so years regard it as an area of systematically false or meaningless statements.

Now, it is my thesis here that the Christ-centered piety of the evangelical tradition provides both the knowledge and the community within which people can find a basis for moral development, because in that tradition they find a solid basis for human life.

We by no means claim that evangelical piety is the *only* Christ-centered piety. That would be historically mistaken and a hindrance to any further inquiry. There are many other pieties that center on Christ and share certain essential elements with evangelicalism. One of the first books that John Wesley published, for example, was a little version of *The Imitation of Christ* by Thomas à Kempis that was called *The Christian Pattern.* An essentially evangelical piety, though not under that name or outward form, has been present in many Christian movements and has often nourished evangelical religion. (We think of the Rhineland Mystics, for example.) Nevertheless, a clearly identifiable tradition of Christ-centered piety characterizes the evangelical movement, and I want to outline its major aspects.

I should acknowledge, before I go on, that the marks of evangelical religion across the ages are not necessarily the ones emphasized today. A recent spokesman for evangelicalism said it had three essential marks: belief in the uniquely divine nature of Jesus, in the Bible as the Word of God, and in the necessity of a new birth. But this post–World War II evangelicalism is clearly a variant on evangelicalism in general.

The three substantive elements of evangelical piety across the ages are, in my opinion, *conviction of sin*, *conversion to a godly life of faith,* and *testimony to the saving work of God in the soul.*

Conviction of sin is no longer a popular topic among evangelicals. It has disappeared for the most part, but that is a quite recent development. Mordecai Ham, the evangelist under whose influence Billy Graham was converted, would preach for weeks in a given location before giving people an opportunity to receive Christ. That was a common practice. Often the mental suffering would become very great and spread to believers. In Savannah, Georgia, the tension drove Christians to become so burdened that they went downtown and rented empty store buildings in order to hold meetings on their own, where they could publicly invite people to receive Christ by giving an "invitation."

Wesley's famous statement, "I must preach law before I preach grace," was the standard. Now it is largely disregarded, if it is known at all. No one would think of actually following it, as used to be the case. Yet, I think, a foundation for evangelical piety, across the ages and even now, remains not only conviction of sin, alienation from God, condemnation, and a sense of eternal loss but also deliverance from *bondage to* sin—from the inability to stop sinning. We still hear a great deal about this, though it is not exactly central.

The evangelical tradition, in such figures as Martin Luther, Richard Baxter, Philip Spener, John Wesley, Charles Finney, and many others, deals at great length with guilt before God and bondage to the practice of sin. Sometimes the tradition, in reaction, verges on perfectionism—one of the ghosts that has haunted many forms of evangelicalism. But conviction of sin remains, in some form, a standard part of Christ-centered piety in the evangelical tradition up to today, though currently involving a great deal of confusion. Without it there is really no problem for the gospel to solve. Can "having a need" play the same role in piety as conviction of sin? "Sin" has totally disappeared as a category of analysis and understanding in contemporary culture. Still, without sin, evangelical religion makes no sense, and the emphasis of that religion upon sin has always been a matter of reproach to it.

The second basic element in evangelicalism, broadly viewed, is *conversion*. This involves both reconciliation and regeneration. The loss of the concept of regeneration characterizes much of evangelical theology today. Often all that is stressed is reconciliation or forgiveness—where even that has not been replaced by Christ "meeting your needs." Sometimes the doctrine of regeneration is totally absorbed in the doctrine of justification. They are straight on identified. But that is *not* characteristic of the tradition generally. If you read not only the popular sources but also the standard theologies, you will see that regeneration, or coming to have a new kind of life ("from above"), is as central to conversion as is forgiveness. Perhaps, indeed, forgiveness is even subordinate to it. You are given new life by grace through faith, and in that process, or in the light of it, your sins are, of course, forgiven. You can't live in God or God in you without forgiveness and reconciliation.

The third element, *testimony*, lives on in many quarters of the evangelical movement, but not, by and large, the way it did traditionally, when testimony was often treated as an integral part of conversion, and belief and confession were inseparable.

Now, along with these three foundational elements of Christ-centered piety in the evangelical tradition, there are some disciplinary aspects—"disciplinary" because they are thought of (to use Wesley's phrase) as "means of grace" or ways of sustaining and developing one's life, not, certainly, as modes of punishment. Primary among these are the public ministry of the Word of God, individual Bible study, prayer, and the ideal of a whole-life discipline and holiness. For broad stretches of evangelical piety, our entire life, no matter what we were doing, was to be a part of our faith in Christ. That was a part of testimony.

This was a valid transposition of the Lutheran idea of the Priesthood of the Believer. It does not primarily mean that any believer could do priestly or religious things, but rather that *whatever* any believer was doing was to be a priestly act unto God. This belief does descend very clearly through much, but not all, of the evangelical tradition.

Finally, piety involves working "the fields white unto harvest." This notion has several meanings, including the *giving* of money and goods. One of the great strengths of Wesley's early little groups was that everyone was supposed to give something, no matter how small. You gave something when you met with your group, and it was used for the benefit of the church, as well for those who had needs of any kind and to help the poor. Today's evangelicals still stand out statistically for their giving. Tithing is a norm, not always met, but also often exceeded.

Working the fields white unto harvest also requires *witness*. That specifically means speaking individually to others about their condition before God and about God's provision for them, as well as involvement in public efforts of evangelization, including missionary outreach across the world. Evangelical piety requires presenting the gospel in all of its connections to life as well as in special public efforts to "reach the lost." In this context one sees why a lively conception of sin remains important.

The final aspect of working the fields white unto harvest is *standing for truth*. This broad category includes "earnestly contending for the faith, once delivered." But it also means standing for what is right and just and good in society, including "speaking truth to power" and political efforts of various kinds.

Those who are living thoughtfully in evangelical circles throughout the generations will very likely believe they have not quite measured up if they are missing in any of these three areas of activity. For evangelicals, Christ-centered piety must always be from the heart and unto the Lord. It is not for the benefit of appearance. It is not to impress people. It is not to impress even God. It is a matter of an honest and transparent heart standing before God and simply calling out, "Just as I am without one plea"—the anthem of modern evangelicalism.

That hymn beautifully expresses this area of transparency as an evangelical ideal: of not trying to make adjustments or impress, but just being who I am and saying that Christ's death on the cross means that now I don't have to be anything other than I am. Since I come to God on such a basis, then I can come to you also, as a human brother and sister, and say, "Just as I am without one plea." We can and should deal with one another on that basis. That is evangelical piety at its best. It is not, of course, unique to evangelicals, and one finds it in many other traditions that display a similar attitude of piety. But evangelicals do emphasize the need for this kind of transparency as a part of the gospel life.

In evangelical piety, broadly conceived, one lives as a disciple of Jesus, and discipleship is, of course, a process of learning and growth. Hence, 2 Peter 3:18 is often quoted among evangelicals: "But grow in the grace and knowledge of our Lord and Savior

Jesus Christ." As a learning process, discipleship means living interactively with his resurrected presence (through his word, his personal presence, and through other people) as we progressively learn *to lead our lives as he would if he were we.* One of the primary problems for *contemporary* evangelicals is that we have lost the concept of discipleship. Among evangelicals generally, it is now assumed that you can be a Christian without being a disciple of Jesus, and many are—or so it seems. In fact, this is widely assumed among Christians far beyond evangelical circles. To be a disciple is to be an apprentice or student of Jesus in Kingdom living. But today evangelicals may even farm the making of disciples out to parachurch organizations and assume that the local church is not necessarily in *that* business.

In fact, we now are somewhat at a loss as to what discipleship is. That is partly related to some theological developments. The teaching of salvation by grace through faith has, in many quarters, brought people to a condition where they really don't know what they are supposed to do. This is no wonder. My background is Southern Baptist. We may preach to you for an hour that there is nothing you can do to be saved, and then sing to you for a half-hour trying to get you to do something ("come forward," profess your faith) to be saved.

Currently we are not only saved by grace; we are paralyzed by it. There is deep confusion. We find it hard to see that grace is not opposed to *effort,* but is opposed to *earning.* Earning and effort are not the same thing. Earning is an attitude, and grace is definitely opposed to that. But it is not opposed to effort. When you see a person who has been caught on fire by grace, you are apt to see some of the most astonishing efforts you can imagine (1 Corinthians 15:10). Of course, the evangelical tradition is filled with effort—for example, the great missionaries (Judson and Carey and others) who went out. Some said to them, "Don't you believe God is going to save who He is going to save?" And they would reply, in effect, "Yes, that's exactly why I am going. I want to be there when it happens." Grace is a tremendous motivator and energizer when you understand and receive it rightly.

Another problem is that evangelicals have often fallen into *legalism* when they try to obey Christ. That is due in large part to the fact that we have emphasized *trying* but not *training* and explains why you may find a fairly high percentage of Pharisees among evangelicals—not necessarily more than among other groups, sacred or secular. When you try to "bless those who curse you," for example, *trying* will prove never to be enough; you have to be *trained* for that. Such training comes under the area of discipleship, but today, generally speaking, we have separated faith in Christ from obedience or fulfillment. There is no available bridge to get from one to the other. That bridge would, of course, be discipleship. If you want to do what Jesus said, you direct your efforts at growing into the kind of person who would, naturally, do those things.

We have lost discipleship largely because, in the evangelical tradition, we have *lost Christ as Teacher*. The idea of Christ as Teacher no longer means much, if anything at all, to evangelicals. This has historical roots in the modernist/fundamentalist controversies of the past century. In those controversies, fundamentalists and conservatives began to understand talk of Christ as Teacher as code for "he is *just* a man." And it was, in fact, often a way of omitting the divinity of Christ. There arose an inward arming against this idea of Christ as Teacher. But of course, if you don't have a teacher, you can't have any students or disciples. We become mere spectators and consumers of holy things, not *participants* in the life Jesus is now living on earth, and we lose meaningful discipline.

Discipline is something we do to enable ourselves to accomplish what we cannot do by direct effort. While the idea and practice of spiritual discipline is very rich in the evangelical tradition, with no living teacher it will not work. So the idea of discipline disappears as a leading idea in evangelicalism because the teacher has disappeared.

We find, then, that evangelicals face a long series of problems in reclaiming, for our time, the power of the long and rich evangelical tradition, thought, and experience as a primary engine to drive the moral transformation of individuals and society. These problems are strongly tied to a further problem about the use of reason and understanding in religion—a problem that also comes to us, in part, as a reaction to the controversies in the nineteenth century and the first part of the twentieth century, but that also reaches much farther into the past. Reason and knowledge were set on the side of the Devil by many evangelicals, and by nearly all people who would be called fundamentalist. They were thus strongly drawn to anti-intellectualism. It was thought that, somehow, what went wrong with those people "over there" (the modernists) was that they started thinking. And perhaps they read too many books, possibly in German or French. There arose an armament against the idea of reason.

Today many evangelicals are trying to reexamine this issue, and they must do so in order to capture Christ as Teacher and begin to think of him as an *intelligent person*—which is now almost impossible for many people, evangelical or not. If you ask evangelicals to pick the smartest man in the world, very few of them will list Jesus Christ. And surely that is sad. It is a modern-day form of Docetism. But if he is divine, would he be dumb? And how can you be a disciple of someone you don't think of as really bright?

Some years ago, there was an ecumenical effort, by evangelicals and others, that took as its slogan "Jesus as Lord." It didn't succeed very well and soon died out because the whole person of Jesus, which is crucial to any Christ-centered piety, was not involved. If you don't think Jesus is smart and highly competent with regard to everything you are involved in, what can you mean by calling him Lord? In a Christ-centered piety, we will have to recapture the greatness of the whole Christ as the object of our faith. We must place our confidence in what Paul called the "boundless riches of Christ" (Ephesians 3:8).

As we do that, the *ideal* character of evangelicalism as a life-transforming force will begin to reemerge. Then we will have reason to think that there might even be some answer to the questions of moral development raised by important leaders such as Derek Bok. He is not alone, of course, in raising those kinds of questions. But where are we to go if we cannot find a knowledge of reality and virtue and goodness at a practical level, as has at times in the past been provided by people in the evangelical tradition?

At the end of his book *The Field of Ethics*, based on his William Belden Noble Lectures for 1899, Harvard philosophy professor George Herbert Palmer listed the names of leaders in the field of ethics at the time and concluded, "Ethics is certainly the study of how life may be full and rich, and not, as is often imagined, how it may be restrained and meager," which, unfortunately, is often the picture that we get from evangelical life today. He continues, "Those words of Jesus—of which Phillips Brooks was so fond—announcing that he had come in order that men might have life and have it abundantly, are the clearest statement of the purposes of both morality and religion, of righteousness on earth and in heaven." This places Jesus Christ, as historically viewed by evangelicals, in his proper context and perspective.

Evangelical thought and tradition make available to human-kind a genuine Saver, one who can be present in today's world to yield life that is abundant and full. I trust and hope and pray that the occasion of this colloquium, under the leadership of people at Harvard, will open the way to a renewal of that kind of depth of life and thought on earth.

CHAPTER 14

Why?

WC/U: Why should we practice the disciplines?

DW: The short answer and the absolute truth is that without discipline nothing of any value can be accomplished. This remains true in the spiritual life with Christ. And the real question is not *whether* we should practice disciplines. We will, and everyone agrees we should. But we need to think carefully about which disciplines we practice and how they should be undertaken.

Much of what we learn in human life is imposed—learning to walk, learning to talk . . . social interactions. Beyond these elemental things, everything that we develop from our lives that is of any value is the result of discipline, of voluntarily chosen and planned activities. Normally, the real making of a person comes from disciplines that only they can choose and impose on themselves. The child who is able to *accept* the disciplines of training may become a great musician. If he doesn't accept them, he won't; you can't impose that, no matter what parents and teachers may wish for.

So, the short answer for "Why discipline?" is that there is no sense of fulfillment, dignity, and quality to life that we can have without discipline. We will grow up with a sense of worthlessness, failure, and become a pest and burden to others. For instance, in nearly every church all the grief that you find basically comes from undisciplined people. If you don't have discipline, there's nothing really to make up for it. The disciplines, with grace, will produce the ideals in our lives that we want: to be able effectively to pray, to love, and so forth.

WC/U: Frequently, in the evangelical church, we've been taught that to be a disciple only requires us to read a portion of scripture daily and to pray. But those two activities easily become meaningless.

DW: Well, you see, in the evangelical churches, the big secret is that few people actually read their Bibles and pray. The reason they don't is because it isn't presented as an essential part of an overall life that is highly desirable and that we must approach in a certain way.

Christians who do read their Bibles often don't *know* their Bibles. The reason why they don't know their Bibles is because they don't really read their Bible as a treatise on *reality*, as something that brings change and transformation of our lives. For instance, many people read their Bibles on a schedule. You really only have to look at them to know what their *aim* is: to read the whole Bible in a year. What that plan is good for is that at the end of the year you can say you read your Bible. It's a legalism. (Of course, some people are significantly benefited by it.)

Back of this lies the idea of portioning out little pieces of something—as if "this is going to be unpleasant," so if you take it in little pieces it will be all right. You would *never* suggest this for *War and Peace* or any other piece of literature. There is absolutely no suggestion in the New Testament that being a disciple consists of reading your Bible and praying regularly. This really does bring us to the heart of the problem for the student today. There is a totally wrong conception of what discipleship is. It's been presented to them basically as attending a church, reading your Bible, praying, and maybe some witnessing, and that's it. Then they come to the university, they look at how they will spend their time, and they think, "I will make discipleship these 'devotional' times." They would be opposed to saying, "My being at the university *is* my discipleship now. My *life* is my discipleship." Or, rather, they just wouldn't know what that meant.

WC/U: If I can fit discipleship in between my reading sixteen chapters of history. . . .

DW: Yes. Many campus ministers try to be very helpful by suggesting something like this, but actually they are perpetuating this idea that if we do certain things at certain times, that will be discipleship. That never has the effect intended—never. Of course, it may be of *some* help.

WC/U: Or we tend to ask a person who's having trouble, "How is your devotional life?"

DW: Yes . . . which has another interesting idea: namely, that your devotional life will keep you out of trouble.

WC/U: My life will be trouble-free . . .

DW: Fascinating idea! The student is in a very special situation; they will never again have this much disposable time. They often think they don't have time for discipleship. The problem is that they do not have their values in order, nor do they know how to order their lives around discipleship. They have these "serious" activities that they've been taught have to do with discipleship, and they cannot muster the energy to pull their lives together in any serious attempt to follow Christ *in all they do*. So, the student thinks that their study of the *Republic,* or of their accounting or chemistry courses, has no intrinsic connection to discipleship at all.

Really, the question of motivation becomes the chief one in reference to practicing the disciplines. Motivation comes from vision, and vision should come from the preaching of the gospel of the Kingdom as an all-encompassing invitation to live life under the rule of God. That means accounting, that means the *Republic,* that even means *Mein Kampf,* or whatever it is you're working on: all serves as an experience of the grace of God daily in all that you do. That then provides the motivation for the disciplines in the same way that involvement in music or sports must provide its own motivation. You begin to enjoy the values of that domain. If you can play a little bit of Beethoven, it's a wonderful gift. It's nourishing; it's sustaining.

When a person begins to step into Kingdom living, she begins to experience the joy of that life, begins to know "Solitude isn't a deprivation. Fasting is an opportunity to learn about how God nourishes us through his Word." Study, service, and church fellowship become different things because they are parts of a whole, and within that whole it's possible to make decisions that would fit in things like Bible study, prayer, and all the things that are indeed valuable. The question is "How can we have a life in which they make sense?"

WC/U: How can I start? What are the steps to entering into the disciplined life?

DW: Again, by *planning* to have a lengthy time alone; you really have to begin there. You never "find" time. You choose to make time.

WC/U: *What do you mean by "lengthy"? A weekend?*

DW: Yes, a weekend is ideal. But you may have to work up to it with an afternoon, or twenty-four hours. Don't be a hero. You have to be sure not to get into something you can't handle. A beginner spending a week alone would probably be nuts by the week's end. But not necessarily. A retreat, or a setting where there can be some alternating between fellowship and solitude, is an excellent place to start. The other part of the advice is: begin thinking of why you really want to do this. It's not necessary to become *completely* clear about this, but you must have *some* clarity. You will have some disappointments. People go on a first retreat and they think they will come back walking on water. Think about what you are wanting and why you are going about this. A good answer is "I'm hoping to learn more about the experience of Christ."

WC/U: *Why is solitude a good place to start?*

DW: With solitude, you begin to unhook yourself from the automatic responses that dominate life around us. Church services don't allow that. You go to church with your family and friends. If you are seeking change there, people don't want to allow that; they want to lock you into who they think you are. You need to go it alone for a while. In that aloneness, you find meaningful, experiential interaction with God. That's a part of what the scripture means when it says, "Seek ye first the Kingdom of God." That means: seek meaningful, experiential interaction with God. The pity is that we don't find very many clear indications of what that interaction consists of in our usual teaching. Meaningful, experiential interaction with God doesn't necessarily happen when we stand and sing, "Seek ye first the Kingdom of God."

WC/U: *It is difficult to understand the connection between motivation and vision. We see Mother Teresa and think, "Yes, I want to be that, but how do I get from where I am now to where she is?"*

DW: I heard a well-known southern California minister asked a similar question, and he replied that Mother Teresa became like that because she prayed and read her Bible. Just like that. Of course, she did pray and read her Bible, but she did so in a context of a life that included, most important, incredible amounts of solitude, silence, service, confession, etc. Most people don't understand the effects of solitude, so they don't understand the reason why we have to have it. What you have got to get to—and this today is regarded as almost sinful—is the point where *you don't have anything to do.*

WC/U: *Well, do I just sit there?*

DW: Simply stated, yes. Of course, you can still breathe or walk about. But this is an application of the law of *Sabbath*—to make us stop *labor,* to make us stop doing anything in the way of work. The reason for that, you see, is that the Kingdom of God is so gentle that as long as we're acting, it usually just lets us go on. We can't turn loose of the world and the place we think we have in it. Isn't it interesting that the Kingdom of God is something that you would have to seek? Solitude is the primary way, and then, of course, silence within that solitude. It's a *harrowing* discipline, in the literal sense.

WC/U: When a person begins practicing silence—such as unplugging the phone, turning off the television and radio, just being quiet for an hour—it can be unnerving after a while. Can silence become enjoyable?

DW: Yes, it is joyous and strengthening. You have to be weaned away from those stimuli and responses that are normal to you, that have made up your life. Then we are able to receive out of silence. Then you will find joy.

WC/U: How did you start investigating the disciplines?

DW: Primarily by reading John Wesley and Charles Finney. Then I began to read very widely in those going before them. I was impressed by their power, which, through my reading, I saw was connected to their behavior, and not just to God's acts *upon* them. I also learned, long ago, that there is a rigorous positive correlation between fasting and the power and effect of preaching and teaching—or just being with people.

WC/U: In what sense is it more powerful?

DW: In the result for good. The difference in the power and effect of the Word spoken is hard to imagine unless you have experienced it. So I will rarely have a regular preaching or teaching appointment where I don't fast for at least half a day. But I fast systematically as well.

WC/U: What is systematically—once a week, every two weeks?

DW: More often that that, but it need not be too long, depending on the discomfort you feel. The general rule for any discipline is: if it's hard to do, you probably need to do it longer and more often.

WC/U: Like lifting weights . . .

DW: Exactly, or learning the piano. You need practice. The disciplines aren't good in and of themselves. The mark of a healthy-minded person is that they take medicine only when it's needed. "Spiritual" reading has also been important to me. One significant reading was Jeremy Taylor's *Holy Living and Holy Dying* . . . he just made overwhelming good sense. You see, there is a kind of cycle of entering into a meaningful interaction with God: read your Bible, read good books, experience in practice what you have been reading about, go back to your Bible, and so on. Our experience involves practicing the disciplines to enable us to act in greater faith. The disciplines are a simple way in which to seek the Kingdom of God. Not to earn it, but to know it. And, of course, finding the Kingdom of God is living the rule and reign of God in our lives.

WC/U: Did you have a support group?

DW: No, I didn't. There were none in my reach. That's where the books helped, and a few individuals. But I can imagine that it would be helpful to have a group. There have been cases of very famous groups, for instance, around St. Francis, Ignatius, St. Philip Neri, Wesley's Holy Club, George Fox's early friends, and today the lifelong group around Billy Graham. But we do need to be careful with groups and not allow them to preempt any part of our soul. We need to avoid thinking about how to describe what happens when you report back to the group. Which brings me to another discipline: secrecy. The Kingdom of God is in secret . . . in the presence of God's secret seeing. All the disciplines are, where possible, to be done in secret, so that no one knows what's going on, such as the praying, fasting, and giving alms (see Matthew 6).

WC/U: How can we keep from slipping into legalism while practicing the disciplines?

DW: That is a great danger, and the first thing is to recognize it as such. Legalism is almost like the air that we breathe in human society. It can be, and often is, secular as well as religious. It comes out of our need to *appear* right in the eyes of other people, or even—should we be so foolish—before God. If we practice confession or "accountability" with particular people, it, along with other disciplines, will help to keep us straight. Matthew 6 addresses our need for others to think well of us. The disciplines teach us how to live without depending on the opinion of others. Do well, and then pray that it will be unknown, and arrange for it to be unknown unless that involves deceit. The disciplines are training for enduring mistakes other may make about us, training for being misunderstood. George Fox said we need to "take people off of men and put them onto Christ." There is nothing more important than that.

Finding the Kingdom of God is seeing and working with His activities in our lives in and around us. The Kingdom of God *is* God-governing, God-acting. To know God-acting we have to put ourselves into everything we do expecting to interact with God there. The student at the university or college can see the hand of God in everything they do. And so can anyone else.

CHAPTER 15

Jesus the Logician

F EW TODAY WILL HAVE SEEN the words "Jesus" and "logician" put together to form a phrase or sentence, unless it would be to *deny* any connection between them at all. The phrase "Jesus the logician" is not ungrammatical, any more than is "Jesus the carpenter." But it feels upon first encounter to be something like a category mistake or error in logical type, such as "Purple is asleep," or, "More people live in the winter than in cities," or, "Do you walk to work or carry your lunch?"

There is in our culture an uneasy relation between Jesus and intelligence, and I have actually heard Christians respond to my statement that Jesus is the most intelligent man who ever lived by saying that it is an oxymoron. Today we automatically position him away from (or even in opposition to) the intellect and intellectual life. Almost no one would consider him to be a *thinker*, addressing the same issues as, say, Aristotle, Kant, Heidegger, or Wittgenstein, and with the same logical method.

Now, this fact has important implications for how we today view his relationship to our world and our life—especially if our work happens to be that of art, thought, research, or scholarship. How could he fit into such a line of work, and lead us in it, if he were logically obtuse? How could we be his disciples at our work, take him seriously as our teacher there, if when we enter our fields of technical or professional competence we must leave him at the door? Obviously some repositioning is in order, and it may be helped along simply by observing his use of logic and his obvious powers of logical thinking as manifested in the gospels of the New Testament.

Now, when we speak of "Jesus the logician" we do not, of course, mean that he developed *theories* of logic, as did, for example, Aristotle and Frege. No doubt he *could* have, if he is who Christians have taken him to be. He could have provided a *Begriffsschrift*, or a *Principia Mathematica,* or alternative axiomatizations of modal logic, or various completeness or incompleteness proofs for various "languages." (He is, presumably, responsible for the order that is represented through such efforts as these.)

He could have, just as he could have handed Peter or John the formulas of relativity physics or the plate tectonic theory of the earth's crust. He certainly could, that is, if he is indeed the one Christians have traditionally taken him to be. But he did not do it, and for reasons that are bound to seem pretty obvious to anyone who stops to think about it. But that, in any case, is not my subject here. When I speak of "Jesus the logician," I refer to his use of logical insights, to his mastery and employment of logical principles in his work as a teacher and public figure.

Now, it is worth noting that those who do creative work or are experts in the field of logical theory are not necessarily more logical or more philosophically sound than those who do not. We might hope that they would be, but they may even be illogical in how they work out their own logical theories. For some reason great powers in theory do not seem to guarantee significantly greater accuracy in practice. Perhaps no person well informed about the history of thought will be surprised at this statement, but for most of us it needs to be emphasized. To have understanding of developed logical theory surely could help one to think logically, but it is not sufficient to guarantee logical thinking, and except for certain rarified cases it is not even necessary. Logical insight rarely depends upon logical theory, though it does depend upon logical relations. The two primary logical relations are implication (logical entailment) and contradiction, and their role in standard forms of argument such as the Barbara syllogism, disjunctive syllogism, modus ponens, and modus tollens—and even in strategies such as reductio ad absurdum—can be fully appreciated, for practical purposes, without rising to the level of theoretical generalization at all.[1]

To be logical no doubt does require an understanding of what implication and contradiction are, as well as the ability to recognize their presence or absence in obvious cases. But it also requires the will to be logical, and then certain personal qualities that make it possible and actual—qualities such as freedom from distraction, focused attention on the meanings or ideas involved in talk and thought, devotion to truth, and willingness to follow the truth wherever it leads via logical relations. All of this in turn makes significant demands upon moral character. Not just on points such as resoluteness and courage, though those are required. A practicing hypocrite, for example, will not find a friend in logic, nor will liars, thieves, murderers, and adulterers. They will be constantly alert to appearances and inferences that may logically implicate them in their wrong actions. Thus, the literary and cinematic genre of *mysteries* is unthinkable without play on logical relations.

Those devoted to defending certain pet assumptions or practices come what may will also have to protect themselves from logic. All of this is, I believe, commonly recognized by thoughtful people. Less well understood is the fact that one can be logical only if one is committed to being logical as a fundamental value. One is not logical by chance, any more than one just happens to be moral. And, indeed, logical consistency is a significant factor in moral character. That is part of the reason why in an age that attacks morality, as ours does, the logical will also be demoted or set aside—as it now is.

Not only does Jesus not concentrate on logical *theory*, but he also does not spell out all the details of the logical structures he employs on particular occasions. His use of logic is always enthymemic, as is common to ordinary life and conversation. His points are, with respect to logical *explicitness*, understated and underdeveloped. The significance of the enthymeme is that it enlists the mind of the hearer or hearers *from the inside*, in a way that full and explicit statement of argument cannot do. Its rhetorical force is, accordingly, quite different from that of fully explicated argumentation, which tends to distance the hearer from the force of logic by locating it outside of his own mind.

Jesus's aim in utilizing logic is not to win battles, but to achieve understanding or insight in his hearers. This understanding only comes from the inside, from the understandings one already has. It seems to "well up from within" one. Thus, he does not follow the logical method one often sees in Plato's dialogues, or the method that characterizes most teaching and writing today. That is, he does not try to make everything so explicit that the conclusion is forced down the throat of the hearer. Rather, he presents matters in such a way that those who wish to know can find their way to, can come to, the appropriate conclusion as something *they* have discovered— whether or not it is something they particularly care for.

"A man convinced against his will is of the same opinion still." Yes, and no doubt Jesus understood that. And so he typically aims at real inward change of view that will enable his hearers to become significantly different as people through the workings of their own intellect. They will have, unless they are strongly resistant to the point of blindness, the famous "eureka" experience, not the experience of being outdone or beaten down.

With these points in mind, let us look at some typical scenes from the gospels—scenes that are, of course, quite familiar, but are now to be examined for the role that distinctively logical thinking plays in them.

Consider Matthew 12:1–8. This contains a teaching about the ritual law, specifically, about the regulations of the temple and the sabbath. Jesus and his disciples are walking through fields of grain—perhaps wheat or barley—on the sabbath, and they are stripping the grains from the stalks with their hands and eating them. The Pharisees accuse them of breaking the law, of being wrongdoers. Jesus, in response, points out that there are conditions in which the ritual laws in question do not apply.

He brings up cases of this that the Pharisees already concede. One is the case (1 Samuel 21:1–6) where David, running for his life, comes to the place of worship and sacrifices supervised by Ahimelich the priest. He asks Ahimelich for food for himself and his companions, but the only food available is bread consecrated in the ritual of the offerings. This bread, as Jesus points out (Matthew 12:4), was forbidden to David by law and was to be eaten (after the ritual) by priests alone. But Ahimelich gives it to David and his men to satisfy their hunger. Hunger as a human need, therefore, may justify doing what ritual law forbids.

Also, Jesus continues (second case), the priests every sabbath in their temple service do more work than sabbath regulations allow: "On the sabbath the priests in the temple break the sabbath and yet are guiltless" (Matthew 12:5). It logically follows, then, that one is not automatically guilty of wrongdoing or disobedience when one does not keep the ritual observances as dictated, in case there is some greater need that must be met. This is something the Pharisees have, by implication, already admitted by accepting the rightness in the two cases Jesus refers to.

The still deeper issue here is the use of law to harm people, something that is not God's intention. Any time ritual and compassion (for example, for hunger) come into conflict, God, who gave the law, favors compassion. That is the kind of God He is. To think otherwise is to misunderstand God and to cast Him in a bad light. Thus, Jesus quotes the prophet Hosea: "But if you had known what this means, 'I desire mercy and not sacrifice' [Hosea 6:61], you would not have condemned the guiltless" (Matthew 12:7; see also 9:13). Thus, the use of logic here is not only to correct the judgment that the disciples (the "guiltless" in this case) must be sinning in stripping the grain and eating it. It is used to draw a further implication about God: God is not the kind of person who condemns those who act to meet a significant need at the expense of a relative triviality in the law. Elsewhere he points out that the sabbath appointed by God was made to serve man, not man to serve the sabbath (Mark 2:27).

Now, the case of sabbath keeping—or, more precisely, of the ritual laws developed by men for sabbath observance—is one that comes up over and over in the gospels, and it is always approached by Jesus in terms of the logical inconsistency of those who claim to practice it in the manner officially prescribed at the time (see, for example, Mark 3:1–3; Luke 13:15–17; John 9:14–16). They are forced to choose between hypocrisy and open inconsistency, and he does sometimes use the word "hypocrisy" of them (see, for example, Luke 13:15), implying that they knew they were being inconsistent and accepted it. In fact, the very idea of hypocrisy implies logical inconsistency. "They say, and do not" what their saying implies (Matthew 23:3). And legalism will always lead to inconsistency in life, if not hypocrisy, for it will eventuate in giving greater importance to rules than is compatible with the principles one espouses (giving greater importance to sacrifice, for example, than to compassion in the case at hand), and also to an inconsistent practice of the rules themselves (for example, leading one's donkey to water on the sabbath, but refusing to have a human being healed of an eighteen-year-long affliction, as in Luke 13:15–16).

Another illustrative case is found in Luke 20:27–40. Here it is the Sadducees, not the Pharisees, who are challenging Jesus. They are famous for rejecting the resurrection (verse 27), and accordingly they propose a situation that, they think, is a reductio ad absurdum of resurrection (Luke 20:28–33). The law of Moses said that if a married man dies without children, the next eldest brother should make the widow his wife, and any children they have will inherit in the line of the older brother. In the "thought experiment" of the Sadducees, the elder of seven sons dies without children from his wife, the next eldest marries her and also dies without children from her, and the next eldest does the same, and so on through all seven brothers. Then the wife dies (small wonder!). The presumed absurdity in the case was that in the resurrection she would be the wife of *all* of them, which was assumed to be an impossibility in the nature of marriage.

Jesus's reply is to point out that those resurrected will not have mortal bodies suited for sexual relations, marriage, and reproduction. They will have bodies like angels do now, bodies of undying stuff. The idea of resurrection must not be taken crudely. Thus, he undermines the assumption of the Sadducees that any resurrection must involve the body and its life continuing *exactly as it does now*. So the supposed impossibility of the woman being in conjugal relations with all seven brothers is not required by resurrection.

Then he proceeds, once again, to develop a teaching about the nature of God, which was always his main concern. Taking a premise that the Sadducees accept, he draws the conclusion that they do not want. That the dead are raised, he says, follows from God's self-description to Moses at the burning bush. God describes Himself in that incident as "the God of Abraham, the God of Isaac, and the God of Jacob" (Luke 20:37; see Exodus 3:16). The Sadducees accept this. But at the time of the burning bush incident, Abraham, Isaac, and Jacob had been long "dead," as Jesus points out. But God is not the God of the dead. That is, a dead person cannot sustain a relation of devotion and service to God, nor can God keep covenant faith with one who no longer exists. In covenant relationship to God one lives (Luke 20:38). One cannot very well imagine the living God communing with a dead body or a nonexistent person and keeping covenant faithfulness with them.

(Incidentally, those Christian thinkers who nowadays suggest that the godly do not exist or are without conscious life, at least, from the time their body dies to the time *it* is resurrected, might want to provide us with an interpretation of this passage.)

Yet another illustration of Jesus's obviously self-conscious use of logic follows upon the one just cited from Luke 20. He would occasionally set teaching puzzles that required the use of logic on the part of his hearers. After the discussion of the resurrection, the Sadducees and the other groups about him no longer have the courage to challenge his powerful thinking (Luke 20:40). He then sets them a puzzle designed to help them understand the Messiah—for whom everyone was looking.

Drawing upon what all understood to be a messianic reference, in Psalm 110, Jesus points out an apparent contradiction: the Messiah is the son of David (admitted by all), and yet David calls the Messiah "Lord" (Luke 20:42–43). How, he asks, can the Messiah be David's son if David calls him Lord? (Luke 20:44). The resolution intended by Jesus is that they should recognize that the Messiah is not simply the son of David, but also of One higher than David, and that he is therefore king in a more inclusive sense than political head of the Jewish nation (Revelation 1:5). The promises to David therefore reach far beyond David, incorporating him and much more. This reinterpretation of David and the Messiah was a lesson learned and used well by the apostles and early disciples (see Acts 2:25–36; Hebrews 5:6; Philippians 2:9–11).

For a final illustration we turn to the use of logic on one of the more didactic occasions recorded in the gospels. The parables and stories of Jesus often illustrate his use of logic, but we will look instead at a well-known passage from the Sermon on the Mount. In his teaching about adultery and the cultivation of sexual lust, Jesus makes the statement, "If your right eye causes you to sin, tear it out and throw it away; it is better for you to lose one of your members than for your whole body to be thrown into hell," and similarly for your right hand (Matthew 5:29–30).

What exactly is Jesus doing here? One would certainly be mistaken in thinking that he is advising anyone to actually dismember himself as a way of escaping damnation. One must keep the context in mind. Jesus is exhibiting the righteousness that goes beyond the "righteousness of the scribes and Pharisees." This latter was a righteousness that took as its goal to not do anything wrong. If not doing anything wrong is the goal, that can be achieved by dismembering yourself and making actions impossible. What you cannot do you certainly will not do. Remove your eye, your hand, etc., therefore, and you will roll into heaven a mutilated stump. The price of dismemberment would be small compared to the reward of heaven. That is the logical conclusion *for one who held the beliefs of the scribes and the Pharisees.* Jesus is urging them to be consistent with their principles and do in practice what their principles imply. He reduces their principle, that righteousness lies in not doing anything wrong, to the absurd, in the hope that they will forsake their principle and see and enter the righteousness that is "beyond the righteousness of the scribes and Pharisees"—beyond, where compassion or love and not sacrifice is the fundamental thing. Jesus, of course, knew that if you dismember yourself you can still have a hateful heart, toward God and toward man. It wouldn't really help toward righteousness at all. That is the basic thing he is teaching in this passage. Failure to appreciate the logic makes it impossible to get his point.

These illustrative scenes from the gospels will already be familiar to any student of scripture. But as we know, familiarity has its disadvantages. My hope is to enable us to see Jesus in a new light: to see him as doing *intellectual* work with the appropriate tools of logic, to see him as one who is both at home in and the master of such work.

We need to understand that Jesus is a *thinker*, that this is not a dirty word but an essential work, and that his other attributes do not preclude thought, but only ensure that he is certainly the greatest thinker of the human race: "the most intelligent person who ever lived on earth." He constantly uses the power of logical insight to enable people to come to the truth about themselves and about God from the inside of their own heart and mind. Quite certainly it also played a role in his own growth in "wisdom" (Luke 2:52).

Often, it seems to me, we see and hear his deeds and words, but we don't think of him as one who *knew how* to do what he did or who really had logical *insight* into the things he said. We don't automatically think of him as a very competent person. He multiplied the loaves and fishes and walked on water, for example, but, perhaps, he didn't *know how* to do it, he just used mindless incantations or prayers. Or he taught on how to be a really good person, but he did not have moral insight and understanding. He just mindlessly rattled off words that were piped into him and through him. Really?

We may take this approach to Jesus because we think that knowledge is *human*, while he was divine. Logic means works, while he is grace. Did we forget something there? Possibly that he also is human? Or that grace is not opposed to effort but to *earning*? But human thought is evil, we are told. How could he think human thought, have human knowledge? So we distance him from ourselves, perhaps intending to elevate him, and we elevate him right out of relevance to our actual lives—especially as they involve the use of our minds. That is why the idea of Jesus as logical, of Jesus the logician, is shocking. And of course, that extends to Jesus the scientist, researcher, scholar, artist, literary person. He just doesn't "fit" in those areas. Today it is easier to think of Jesus as a TV evangelist than as an author, teacher, or artist in the contemporary context. But now really!—if he were divine, would he be dumb, logically challenged, uninformed in *any* area? Would he not instead be the *greatest* of artists or speakers? Paul was only being consistent when he told the Colossians that in Christ "are hidden all the treasures of wisdom and knowledge" (2:3). Except for what exactly?

There is in Christian educational circles today a great deal of talk about "integration of faith and learning." Usually it leads to little solid result. This is in part due to the fact that it is, at this point in time, an extremely difficult intellectual task, which cannot be accomplished by ritual language and the pooh-poohing of difficulties. But an even deeper cause of the difficulty is the way we automatically tend to think of Jesus himself. It is not just in what we *say* about him, but in how he comes before our minds: how we automatically position him in our world, and how in consequence we position ourselves. We automatically think of him as having nothing essentially to do with "profane" knowledge, with learning and logic, and therefore we find ourselves on our own in such areas. He cannot go there.

We should, however, understand that Jesus would be perfectly at home in any professional context where good work is being done today. He would, of course, be a constant rebuke to all the proud self-advancement and the contemptuous treatment of others that go on in professional circles. In this as in other respects, our professions are aching for his presence. If we truly see him as the premier thinker of the human race—and who *else* would be that?—then we are also in position to honor him as the most knowledgeable person in *our* field, whatever that may be, and to ask his cooperation and assistance with everything we have to do.

Catherine Marshall somewhere tells of a time she was trying to create a certain design with some drapes for her windows. She was unable to get the proportions right to form the design she had in mind. She gave up in exasperation and, leaving the scene, began to mull the matter over in prayer. Soon ideas as to how the design could be achieved began to come to her, and before long she had the complete solution. She learned that Jesus is maestro of interior decorating.

Such stories are familiar from many areas of human activity, but quite rare in the areas of art and intellect. For lack of an appropriate understanding of Jesus, we come to do our work in intellectual, scholarly, and artistic fields *on our own*. We do not have confidence (otherwise known as faith) that he can be our leader and teacher in matters we spend most of our time working on. Thus, our efforts often fall far short of what they should accomplish and may even have less effect than the efforts of the godless, because we undertake them only with the "arm of the flesh." Our faith in Jesus Christ rises no higher than that. We do not see him as he really is, maestro of all good things.

Here I have only been suggestive of a dimension of Jesus that is commonly overlooked. This is no thorough study of that dimension, but it deserves such study. It is one of major importance for a healthy faith in him—especially today, when the authoritative institutions of our culture, the universities and the professions, omit him as a matter of course. Once one knows what to look for in the gospels, however, one will easily see the thorough, careful, and creative employment of logic throughout his teaching activity. Indeed, this employment must be identified and appreciated if what he is saying is to be understood. Only then can his intellectual brilliance be appreciated and he be respected as he deserves.

An excellent way of teaching in Christian schools would therefore be to require all students to do extensive logical analyses of Jesus's discourses. This should go hand in hand with the other ways of studying his words, including devotional practices such as memorization or lectio divina and the like. It would make a substantial contribution to the integration of faith and learning.

While such a concentration on logic may sound strange today, that is only a reflection on our current situation. It is quite at home in many of the liveliest ages of the church.

John Wesley speaks for the broader Christian church across time and space, I think, in his remarkable treatise "An Address to the Clergy." There he discusses at length the qualifications of an effective minister for Christ. He speaks of the necessity of a good knowledge of scripture, and then adds,

> *Some knowledge of the sciences also, is, to say the least, equally expedient. Nay, may we not say, that the knowledge of one (whether art or science), although now quite unfashionable is even necessary next, and in order to, the knowledge of Scripture itself? I mean logic. For what is this, if rightly understood, but the art of good sense? of apprehending things clearly, judging truly, and reasoning conclusively? What is it, viewed in another light, but the art of learning and teaching; whether by convinc-*

ing or persuading? What is there, then, in the whole compass of science, to be desired in comparison of it?

Is not some acquaintance with what has been termed the second part of logic (metaphysics), if not so necessary as this, yet highly expedient (1.) In order to clear our apprehension (without which it is impossible either to judge correctly, or to reason closely or conclusively), by ranging our ideas under general heads? And (2.) In order to understand many useful writers, who can very hardly be understood without it?[2]

Later in this same treatise Wesley deals with whether we are, as ministers, what we ought to be. "Am I," he asks,

a tolerable master of the sciences? Have I gone through the very gate of them, logic? If not, I am not likely to go much farther when I stumble at the threshold. Do I understand it so as to be ever the better for it? To have it always ready for use; so as to apply every rule of it, when occasion is, almost as naturally as I turn my hand? Do I understand it at all? Are not even the moods and figures [of the syllogism] above my comprehension? Do not I poorly endeavour to cover my ignorance, by affecting to laugh at their barbarous names? Can I even reduce an indirect mood to a direct; an hypothetic to a categorical syllogism? Rather, have not my stupid indolence and laziness made me very ready to believe, what the little wits and pretty gentlemen affirm, "that logic is good for nothing"? It is good for this at least (wherever it is understood), to make people talk less; by showing them both what is, and what is not, to the point; and how extremely hard it is to prove any thing. Do I understand metaphysics; if not the depths of the Schoolmen, the subtleties of Scotus or Aquinas, yet the first rudiments, the general principles, of that useful science?

Have I conquered so much of it, as to clear my apprehension and range my ideas under proper heads; so much as enables me to read with ease and pleasure, as well as profit, Dr. Henry Moore's Works, Malebranche's *Search after Truth,* and Dr. Clarke's Demonstration of the Being and Attributes of God?[3]

I suspect that such statements will be strange, shocking, even outrageous or ridiculous to leaders of ministerial education today. But readers of Wesley and other great ministers of the past, such as Jonathan Edwards or Charles Finney, will easily see, if they know what it is they are looking at, how much use those ministers made of careful logic. Similarly for the great Puritan writers of an earlier period, and for later effective Christians such as C. S. Lewis and Francis Schaeffer. They all make relentless use of logic, and to great good effect. With none of these great teachers is it a matter of trusting logic instead of relying upon the Holy Spirit. Rather, they well knew, it is simply a matter of meeting the conditions along with which the Holy Spirit chooses to work. In this connection it will be illuminating to carefully examine the logical structure and force of Peter's discourse on the day of Pentecost (Acts 2).

Today, in contrast, we commonly depend upon the emotional pull of stories and images to move people. We fail to understand that, in the very nature of the human mind, emotion does not reliably generate belief or faith, if it generates it at all. Not even "seeing" does, unless you know what you are seeing. It is understanding, insight, that generates belief. In vain do we try to change people's hearts or character by moving them to do things in ways that bypass their understanding.

Some time ago, one who is regarded as a great teacher of homiletics was emphasizing the importance of stories in preaching. It was on a radio program. He remarked that a leading minister in America had told him recently that he could preach the same series of sermons each year, and change the illustrations, and no one would notice it. This was supposed to point out, with some humor, the importance of stories to preaching. What it really pointed out, however, was that the cognitive content of the sermon was never heard—if there was any to be heard—and did not matter.

Paying careful attention to how Jesus made use of logical thinking can strengthen our confidence in Jesus as master of the centers of intellect and creativity and can encourage us to accept him as master in all of the areas of intellectual life in which we may participate. In those areas we can, then, be his disciples, not disciples of the current movements and glittering personalities who happen to dominate our field in human terms. Proper regard for him can also encourage us to follow his example as teachers in Christian contexts. We can learn from him to use logical reasoning at its best, as he works with us. When we teach what he taught in the manner he taught it, we will see his kind of result in the lives of those to whom we minister.[4]

BOOKS ON
SPIRITUAL LIVING:
VISIONS AND
PRACTICES

CHAPTER 16

Letters by a Modern Mystic
by Frank C. Laubach

RANK C. LAUBACH (1884–1970) is one of our greatest examples of a modern-day disciple of Jesus living the interactive life of the Kingdom in both the hidden places of earth and in a worldwide ministry of innovation and influence for his Master. He demonstrates in a very striking way how those who are faithful in small things are given responsibility over much as they grow in character and understanding.

A Pennsylvanian trained at Princeton, Union Theological Seminary, and Columbia University (PhD in sociology, 1915), Laubach went to the Philippines under the American Board of Foreign Missions. After fourteen years of successful teaching, writing, and administration at Cagayn and Manila, he realized in 1929 his longstanding ambition of settling among the fierce Moros, an Islamic tribe on Mindanao. There, in the village of Lanao, he underwent a remarkable series of experiences of God and simultaneously developed a technique for reducing the Moro language to writing, with symbols closely correlated to their spoken words. This not only made it possible to teach them to read in only a few hours, but permitted them immediately to teach others. The famous "Each One Teach One" program was born, and with the generalization of his linguistic methods, the foundation was laid for his worldwide efforts to promote literacy, beginning with India in 1935. During his last thirty years, Laubach was an international presence in literacy, religious, and governmental circles. His personal contacts with President Truman were thought to be partly responsible for "point four" in Truman's inaugural address of 1949, sponsoring a "bold new program . . . for the improvement and growth of underdeveloped areas" of the world.

Letters by a Modern Mystic, first published in 1937, consists of excerpts from a series of letters to his father in the United States, dated from January 3, 1930, through January 2, 1932. Though derived from letters, this book is in the lineage of St. Augustine's *Confessions,* being a narrative of Laubach's ascent into the life of active union with God. His psychological and theological training enabled him to observe and describe his experiences in discipleship with an extraordinary degree of clarity, making them accessible for the benefit of other disciples.

Major themes in this little work (and other writings from his life) are

> Submission to the will of God means cooperation with God in the moment-to-moment activities that make up our daily existence.
>
> This cooperation is achieved through continuous inner conversation with God.
>
> That conversation in turn is, from our side, a matter of keeping God constantly before the mind.
>
> One learns to keep God constantly in mind by experimentation, by trying various experiential devices, until the habit of constant God-thought is established.
>
> Then God permeates the self and transforms its world and its relations to others into God's field of constant action, in

which all of the promises of Christ's gospel are realized in abundance of life.

It is possible for all people under all conditions to establish this habit if they make constant effort and experiment within their peculiar circumstances to discover how it can be done.

How did he come to understand these things through the course of his experience? Two years prior to his transforming experiences of 1930, on Mindanao, Laubach found himself profoundly dissatisfied in the realization that after fifteen years as a Christian minister he still was not living his days "in minute by minute effort to follow the will of God." He then began trying to "line up" his actions with the will of God every few minutes. His confidants at the time told him he was seeking the impossible. But in 1929 he began to try living *all* his waking moments "in conscious listening to the inner voice, asking without ceasing, 'What, Father, do you desire said? What, Father, do you desire done this minute?'" In his view, this is exactly what Jesus did.

Laubach did not fall into the trap of *merely trying* to achieve his goal. Rather, he understood the necessity of *learning how*, of spiritual method. He was, in fact, a very subtle and realistic experimentalist and regarded himself as fortunate to be living in a "day when psychological experimentation has given a fresh approach to our spiritual problems." Thus, he experimented for a few days by taking enough time from each hour to give intensive thought to God. Again, "disgusted with the pettiness and futility of my unled self," he experimented with "feeling God in each movement by an act of will—willing that He shall direct these fingers that now strike this typewriter—willing that He shall pour through my steps as I walk." Again, he wished to "compel his mind" to "open straight out to God." But to attain this mental state often required a long time in the morning. Therefore, he determined not to get out of bed "until that mind set, that concentration upon God, is settled." He found that great determination was required to keep the mind on God. But he also found it quickly getting easier and hoped that "after a while, perhaps, it will become a habit, and the sense of effort will grow less."

In the most subtle passage in these letters—so far as the "mechanisms" of holding God before the mind are concerned—Laubach deals with the question of whether it is *possible* to have contact with God all the time. Can we think His thoughts all the time? *Must* there not be periods when other things push God out? Laubach's response to this issue should be fully quoted, for it gives us the heart of his understanding of the constant conscious hold on God for the disciple of Jesus. Admitting that he once thought there must be periods when God is excluded, he continues,

> But I am changing my view. We can keep two things in mind at once. Indeed we cannot keep one thing in mind more than half a second. Mind is a flowing something. It oscillates. Concentration is merely the continuous return to the same problem from a million angles. We do not think of one thing. We always think of the relationship of at least two things, and more often of three or more things simultaneously. So my problem is this: Can I bring God back in my mind-flow every few seconds so that God shall always be in my mind as an after-image, shall always be one of the elements in every concept and percept?
>
> I choose to make the rest of my life an experiment in answering this question.

The tremendous results of this experiment are found in the narrative of these letters. They are elaborated more systematically and practically, perhaps, in his *Game with Minutes* (1961), where the method is reduced to calling God to mind for at least one second out of each minute. But the quotation given contains the psychological principles back of Laubach's method for achieving active union with God, constantly abiding in the abundant life.

Within weeks of beginning his experiments he began to notice differences. By the end of January 1930, and with much still to learn about his method, he had gained a sense of being carried along by God through the hours, of cooperation with God in little things, which he had never felt before. "I need something, and turn around to find it waiting for me. I must work, . . . but there is God working along with me." He discovered by March 9 that "*This hour* can be heaven. *Any* hour for *any* body can be rich with God." In a manner familiar to the mystics of all ages, we find him saying to God, "And God, I scarce see how one could live if his heart held more than mine has had from Thee this past two hours." He experienced difficulties and failures in maintaining his consciousness of God, but in the week ending May 24 he began to experience a further dimension in his conversations with God. In a moment of immersion in natural beauty, "I let my tongue go loose and from it there flowed poetry far more beautiful than any I ever composed. It flowed without pausing and without ever a failing syllable for a half hour." This brought him a deeper awareness of God in beauty and in love.

Reflecting upon the results of two months of strenuous effort to keep God in mind every minute, he exclaims, "This concentration upon God is *strenuous,* but everything else has ceased to be so!" That was especially true of his relations to the people of the Moros tribe, who, seeing the difference in him, took him entirely into their hearts and lives, loving, trusting, and helping him without regard to their cultural and religious differences. Two of the leading Muslim priests went about the area telling their people that Laubach would help them to know God. He never pretended to be anything but a follower of Jesus, but he studied the Bible and the Koran with the priests and the people and prayed in their services with them. Observing this, one priest said, "He is Islam." He replied, "A friend of Islam." But the Islamic emphasis upon constant submission seems to have been one factor prompting him to develop his way of being in constant contact with God. He could not endure to see his practice as a Christian fall below the profession of Islam. The inner transformation was substantial and with real outward effects. "God does work a change. The moment I turn to him it is like turning on an electric current which I feel through my whole being." There is a "real presence" that affects other people directly, and that also makes intercessory prayer an exercise of substantial power in cooperation with God.

In the letters after the mid-1930s there is a different range of concerns, which predominantly have to do with various practical aspects of the life in union with God. These are further elaborated and beautifully concretized for the varying conditions of life in *Game with Minutes*—which, of course, was written to guide others, as the *Letters* were not.

Because of Laubach's immense involvement with worldwide social problems, he came to be generally known for his work, not for his inner life. Many of those who have written about him say little about his spiritual side and obviously do not know what to make of it. But his own words and writings (he published more than fifty books) reveal that he remained primarily a spiritual man—fundamentally living from his moment-to-moment relation to God—to the end of his days. He knew this relation in a way that did not bear many of the external trappings conventionally associated with spirituality. But to observe his effect is to see that he was truly one of those born of the Spirit, of the "wind" that invisibly produces visible results (John 3:8).

Further Reading

Edwards, Gene, ed. *Practicing His Presence: Frank Laubach and Brother Lawrence* (Christian Books, 1973). An instructive comparison.

Frank C. Laubach, Man of Prayer (Laubach Literacy International, 1990). Contains most of Laubach's writings on the spiritual life with Jesus.

Laubach, Frank C. *Letters by a Modern Mystic,* foreword by Alden H. Clark, edited and compiled by Constance E. Padwick (New Readers Press, 1955; first published in 1937).

———. "Christ Liveth in Me" *and* "Game with Minutes" (Fleming H. Revell Co., 1961). A practical guide to living with God in mind.

———. *Prayer, the Mightiest Force in the World* (Fleming H. Revell Co., 1951).

———. *The World Is Learning Compassion* (Fleming H. Revell Co., 1958). Chapter 7 deals with Truman's "point four."

Medary, Marjorie. *Each One Teach One: Frank Laubach, Friend to Millions* (Longmans, Green & Co., 1954). An account of Laubach's linguistic methods.

CHAPTER 17

The Interior Castle of
Teresa of Avila

I FIRST STUDIED TERESA OF AVILA's *Interior Castle* twenty or so years ago, after many years of efforts to understand, live, and communicate what the spiritual life portrayed in the Bible was meant to be. I had, by then, found many helpful companions on the Way, spread across time and space and from many "denominational distinctives." But this book and this author immediately announced themselves as a unique presence of God in my life. The book provided instruction on a living relationship with God that I had found nowhere else. I think it very likely that you will experience the same refreshing shock as I did when you read this book.

The first thing that Teresa helped me with was appreciation of the dignity and value—indeed, the vast reality—of the human soul. Emphasis upon the wickedness and neediness of the human being, a dominant theme in my upbringing, tends to submerge our awareness of our greatness and our worth to God. That emphasis in turn inclines us toward thinking of ourselves as *nothing*, and toward mistaking our lostness and vileness for *nothingness*, a mere vacuum, rather than seeing it as the desolation of a *splendid ruin.*

Teresa urges us to start on the path to transformation by "considering our soul to be like a castle made entirely out of a diamond or of very clear crystal, in which there are many rooms." We are meant to occupy every room or "dwelling place" with God and thereby to become the radiant beings that he intends. Teresa makes clear what lies half-concealed upon the pages of the Bible and in the lives of the "great ones" for Christ—*that I am an unceasing spiritual being, with an eternal destiny in God's great universe.* We may be far from God's will, but we must know "that it is possible in this exile for so great a God to commune with such foul-smelling worms; and, on seeing this, come to love a goodness so perfect and a mercy so immeasurable."

The "rooms" in the interior castle are *ways of living in relation* to the God who made us and seeks us. Teresa's superiors had ordered her to write on prayer. And so she does, but prayer understood precisely as a way of living, not as an occasional exercise. This book, and others such as *The Way of the Pilgrim,* helped me to understand what it is to live a *life* of prayer. I learned from it what it means to live in communication with God, not just speaking to him, but listening and acting. Most of what I know about the phenomenology of God speaking to us, I learned from studying and putting into practice what Teresa says in Dwelling Place Six, Chapter Three. It is still, I think, the best treatment ever written of what it is like for God to *speak to* his children.

Another thing I came to see more clearly from studying this book was why things go as they do in the lives of professing Christians. There is still today not much good information on this. But if you will look at ordinary "church life" with Dwelling Places One through Four in hand, you will be able to understand a huge amount of what is really going on, and of what to expect, for good and for ill, and you will be able to give good counsel and direction to yourself and others as you go through the process of life together. You will realize that Teresa is an absolute master of the spiritual life and possesses an amazing depth and richness of spiritual theology. Yet there is no stuffiness or mere "head knowledge" in her at all. She has remarkable freedom to be experimental and to say, "Now, I can't really explain this to you," and to go ahead and say astonishingly illuminating things anyway. You can put what she says to the test.

Back of all this instruction is the fact, which was very important for my particular background, that there is a reliable order and sequence to growth in the spiritual life. This is built into her model of the "castle" of the soul. "Now," she in effect says, "this is the layout, this is what is to be gone through, here is where you start, here are some things to do, and here is what you may expect to happen and what it means." And she conveys all this wisdom with an appealing humble, experimental tone.

Finally, Dwelling Places Five through Seven proved to be, for me, the finest treatments of union with Christ and with God that I have found in spiritual literature. There are other helpful things, in this connection, such as James Stewart's *A Man in Christ,* but for the phenomenology, the descriptive analysis of the details of what it is really like, nothing has ever surpassed Teresa's *Castle.* Union with Christ—in regeneration, justification, sanctification, and glorification—is of all themes the one in most need of recovery today. And Teresa's entire treatment of redemption in the spiritual life with Christ is unsurpassed and unlikely to be surpassed in the future.

One of the unfortunate things that has happened to the latter stages of *The Interior Castle,* and even to the book as a whole, is that people have tried to read it as if it were an "interfaith," and not a distinctively Christian, portrayal of "mystic union." We certainly understand why one might, today, attempt such a reading. But to do this is to miss its substance, deprive it of its context, and make it unprofitable for those whose faith is in Christ and his Father as well as for most others. Of course, anyone is free to take what they can from this book, but to dismiss its particularity will leave little to genuinely assist the reader to walk with God.

A word about how to read this book. It is not a model of easy reading, judged by today's standards, and must be approached as if you were mining for treasure—which you are. First, read it non-stop—just push ahead—to get a view of the whole. Mark themes and divisions clearly as you go, and at the end sketch out the outline. This is crucial for understanding Teresa's project as a teacher. Then go back and read slowly from beginning to end. This time mark striking passages for further study. Then meditatively dwell on those passages, not necessarily from beginning to end, but in the order your heart and mind call you to. Call upon "His Majesty" to assist you as he assisted Teresa. And the diamond castle that is your soul will increasingly glow with the divine presence.

CHAPTER 18

Invitation to Solitude and Silence
by Ruth Haley Barton

BLAISE PASCAL, the remarkable scientist, theologian, and
Christian of the seventeenth century, acutely remarked in
his *Pensees,* or *Thoughts,* (section 136), that "all the un-
happiness of men arises from one single fact, that they cannot stay
quietly in their own room." The reason for this inability, he found,
is the "natural poverty of our feeble and mortal condition, so miserable that nothing can comfort us when we think of it closely." So
we have to be careful not to "think of it closely." This we manage
by what Pascal calls "diversion." We require things to distract us
from ourselves: "hence it comes people so much love noise and
stir; hence it comes that the prison is so horrible a punishment;
hence it comes that the pleasure of solitude is a thing incompre-
hensible."

True, Pascal observes, we have "another secret instinct, a rem-
nant of the greatness of our original nature, which teaches that
happiness in reality consists only in rest, and not in being stirred
up." This instinct conflicts with the drive to diversion, and we develop the confused idea that leads people to aim at rest through

excitement, "and always to fancy that the satisfaction which they do not have will come to them, if, by surmounting whatever difficulties confront them, they can thereby open the door to rest."

Of course, it doesn't come that way. That is the fallacy in the thinking that all one needs is more time. Unless a deeper solution is found, "more time" will just fill up in the same way as the time we already have. The way to liberation and rest lies through a decision and a practice.

The decision is to release the world and your fate—including your reputation and "success"—into the hands of God. This is not a decision to not act at all, though in some situations it may come to that. It is, rather, a decision concerning *how* you will act: you will act always in dependence upon God.

You will not take charge of outcomes. You will do your part, of course, but "your part" will always be chastened by a sense of who is God—not you!

When King Saul assumed the priestly role and offered sacrifices rather than wait for Samuel (1 Samuel 13:8–12), he decided to "make things happen." He trusted the "arm of the flesh" or natural abilities to get his way. With almost no exception, that was the way of the kings in the Old Testament. But it isn't just for kings. The choice to do what we know to be wrong is always of this nature.

Now, a decision to release the world and our fate to God runs contrary to everything within and around us. We have been "had" by a system of behavior that was here before we got here and seeps into every pore of our being. "Sin," Paul tells us, "was in the world" even before the Law came. It is a massive social presence that forms us internally as well as pressures us externally. Hence, we must find help. We must learn to choose things we can do that will meet with God's actions of grace to break us out of the system that permeates us. These "things" are the disciplines for life in the Spirit, well known from Christian history but much avoided and misunderstood. For those who do not understand our desperate situation, these disciplines look strange or even harmful. But they are absolutely necessary for those who would find rest for their soul in God and not live the distracted existence Pascal so accurately portrays.

Those who are capable of "staying quietly in their own room" are (barring some abnormal condition) persons who have found a good that is sufficient to them and who are unthreatened by anything that might happen. The tendencies to take charge of the world that inhabited their physical and spiritual dimensions no longer have power to govern them or upset them. They have learned by experience and grace that all is perfectly safe in God's hands. Now they can be active, if that is called for, but even then they act with settled love, joy, and peace.

Solitude and silence are the most radical of the disciplines for the spiritual life because they most directly attack the sources of human misery and wrongdoing. To be in solitude is to choose to do nothing. For extensive periods of time. All accomplishment is given up. One learns "hands off." Silence is required to complete solitude, for until we enter quietness, including not listening and speaking, the world still lays hold of us. When we go into solitude and silence, we even stop making demands upon God. It is enough that God is God and we are His. We learn we have a soul, that God is here, that this world is "my Father's world."

When we practice solitude and silence adequately, this knowledge of God progressively replaces the rabid busyness and self-importance that drive most human beings, including the religious ones. It comes to possess us no matter where we are. We no longer need to be in outward solitude and silence in order for them to be in us. Now, whatever we do, "in word or deed, [we do] in the name of the Lord Jesus, giving thanks to God the Father through him" (Colossians 3:17). And that is not another job on top of everything else we have to do. It is not, really, something we have to think to do. For it is who we have become. We still need to attend to solitude and silence, cultivating them, from time to time renewing their depth and strength by going alone and being quiet. But we carry them with us wherever we go.

In the contemporary context (especially the religious context), someone needs to tell us about solitude and silence—just to let us know there are such things. Someone then needs to tell us it's okay to enter them. Someone needs to tell us how to do it, what will happen when we do, and how we go on from there. For Ruth Barton, it was her spiritual director. Now Ruth does that for you.

If you would really like to know the "sabbath rest appropriate for the people of God" (Hebrews 4:9), then make the decision to leave all outcomes to God and enter the practice of solitude and silence with Ruth Barton as your guide. As you do so, call upon Jesus to be with you, and trust him for that. In a relatively short period of time, you will come to know the "rest unto your souls" promised by him who is meek and lowly of heart. It will become the easy and unshakable foundation for your life and your death.

CHAPTER 19

When God Moves In

My Experience with
Deeper Experiences of Famous Christians

T HE ONE BOOK OTHER THAN the Bible that has most influenced me is a little-known book by James Gilchrist Lawson called *Deeper Experiences of Famous Christians*. It was first published in 1911 by the Warner Press of Anderson, Indiana, and was most recently republished in 2000 by Barbour Publishing of Uhrichsville, Ohio.

From a literary or scholarly point of view, the book is of little distinction, which perhaps explains why it is not widely known and seems never to have been widely read or influential. But, given to me in 1954 by a college classmate, Billy Glenn Dudley, it entered my life at a very appropriate time, and, perhaps even more important, it opened to me inexhaustible riches of Christ and his people through the ages. This brought before me, in turn, a world of profound Christian literature of much greater significance for the understanding and practice of life in Christ than that book itself.

The peculiar doctrinal slant of the author led him to interpret "deeper experiences" almost entirely in terms of the filling with, or baptism in, the Holy Spirit. That is an unfortunate grid to place upon the deeper experiences of famous or not-so-famous Christians, as becomes quite clear from the "experiences" of the individuals described in the book. But, fortunately, that peculiar slant did not hinder the author from going, in considerable detail, into what actually happened in the lives of a wide range of outstanding followers of Christ—few of whom would have shared anything close to his view of the relationship between filling or baptism and deeper experiences of God.

The book begins with discussions of biblical characters, from Enoch to the Apostle Paul. Then, interestingly, it takes up certain "Gentile Sages" (Greek, Persian, and Roman), who are also described as under the influence of God's Holy Spirit. Then a section is devoted to outstanding Christians of the early centuries of the church, and, finally, a section (very brief) to "Reformed Churches" and the Reformation period.

The first individual selected by Lawson for a separate chapter was Girolamo Savonarola (born 1452), a major precursor of the Protestant Reformation. What most struck me about Savonarola —and I truly was *smitten*—was his drive toward *holiness*, toward a different and a supernatural kind of life—a life "from above"— and his readiness to sacrifice all to achieve such a life. Indeed, *this* is what stood out in all of the people Lawson dealt with in his book. And the deeper experiences that brought them forward on their way clearly were not all fillings, or baptisms, with the Holy Spirit, though no doubt the Spirit was always involved and genuine fillings and baptisms occurred.

The experiences of these people did from time to time have the character of a filling or baptism, but more often than not they were moments of *realization,* of extreme clarity of insight into profound truth, together with floods of feeling arising therefrom. These experiences often were what George Fox called "openings," and they went right to the bone and changed the life forever.

Thus, of John Bunyan, Lawson writes, "Bunyan's complete deliverance from his dreadful doubts and despair came one day while he was passing through a field. Suddenly the sentence fell upon his soul, '*Thy righteousness is in heaven.*' By the eye of faith he seemed to see Jesus, his righteousness, at God's right hand. He says, 'Now did my chains fall off my legs indeed; I was loosed from my afflictions and irons; my temptations also fled away; so that, from that time, those dreadful Scriptures of God left off to trouble me! Now went I also home rejoicing, for the grace and love of God.' "[1]

I think the book's effect on me will be better understood if we indicate the individuals singled out for chapter-length treatment. After Savanarola came Madam Guyon, François Fenelon, George Fox, John Bunyan, John Wesley, George Whitefield, John Fletcher, Christmas Evans, Lorenzo Dow, Peter Cartwright, Charles G. Finney, Billy Bray, Elder Jacob Knapp, George Müller, A. B. Earle, Frances Ridley Havergal, A. J. Gordon, D. L. Moody, General William Booth, and, in the final chapter, "Other Famous Christians" (Thomas à Kempis, William Penn, Dr. Adam Clarke, William Bramwell, William Carvosso, David Brainerd, Edward Payson, Dorothea Trudel, Pastor John Christolph Blumhardt, Phoebe Palmer, and P. P. Bliss).

Now, clearly this is a very selective and not well-balanced list of "famous Christians." But that was not something that bothered me as I took up the book and studied it. In fact, that these were, by and large, quite ordinary people only impressed upon me all the more that the amazing life into which they were manifestly led could be *mine.* I had been raised in religious circles of very fine people where the emphasis had been exclusively on faithfulness to right beliefs and upon bringing others to profess those beliefs.

Now, that, of course, is of central importance. But when that *alone* is emphasized, the result is a dry and powerless religious life, no matter how sincere, and one constantly vulnerable to temptations of all kinds.

Therefore, to see actual invasions of human life by the presence and action of God, right up into the twentieth century, greatly encouraged me to believe that the life and promises given in the person of Christ and in scripture were meant for us today. I saw that ordinary individuals who *sought* the Lord would find Him real—actually, that He would come to them and convey His reality. It was clear that these "famous Christians" were not seeking experiences, not even experiences of the filling or baptism of the Spirit. They were seeking the Lord, His Kingdom, and His holiness (Matthew 6:33).

Seeking was clearly, from the lives portrayed, a major part of life in Christ. The "doctrinal correctness alone" view of Christianity was, in practice, one of nonseeking. It was basically one of "having arrived," not of continuous seeking, and the next essential stop on its path was heaven after death. But in the light of these "famous Christians," it became clear to me that the path of constant seeking, as portrayed in the Bible (for example, Philippians 3:7–15; Colossians 3:1–17; 2 Peter 1:2–11; etc.), was the life of faith intended for us by God. Salvation by grace through faith was a life, not just an outcome, and the earnest and unrelenting pursuit of God was not "works salvation" but the natural expression of the faith in Christ that saves. Constant discipleship, with its constant seeking for *more* grace and life, was the only sensible response to confidence in Jesus as the Messiah. And the natural (supernatural) accompaniment of that response would, of course, be intermittent but not infrequent experiences of God, some deeper and some not so deep.

Now, "deeper" also meant "broader." Lawson was remarkably unbiased in his selection of the "famous Christians," and this taught me a lot. The individuals selected for presentation ranged very broadly as to cultural and denominational connections. There were a lot of Baptists in the group, which was my own denominational background. That helped me. But there were also Catholics, Anglicans, Methodists, Salvation Army, and others.

Seeing that the experience of God in the calling to holiness and power did not respect sectarian boundaries taught me that I should disregard a lot of things that make for doctrinal and practical insularity in others and place no weight upon them for myself.

It taught me, in Paul's lovely image, to distinguish the treasure from the vessel (2 Corinthians 4:7) and to attend to the treasure: Christ living in the individual life, and the individual living into obedience to Christ. The blessing of God has a natural tendency among men to create denominations, but denominations have no tendency to uniquely foster the blessing of God on anyone. We can and often should honor a denomination or tradition because God has blessed those within it. But it, after all, is the vessel and not the treasure. And we humbly acknowledge this to be true of our vessel as well.

The hunger for holiness, and for power to stand in holiness, to the blessing of multitudes of people, also knows no social or economic boundaries. This too was very important to me and was made brilliantly clear in the lives of the "famous Christians," many of whom were of no standing among humanity or disowned their standing. Not only did that give me hope personally, but it opened afresh the events of scripture for me and showed for modern times how "uneducated and ordinary men" (Acts 4:13) could bring the knowledge and reality of God to the world. It showed how God and one individual, no matter how insignificant in the eyes of men, could make a great difference for good. I resolved that should anything come of my life and ministry it would not be because of my efforts to make that happen.

As I moved on from Lawson's book to study the works of these and many other "famous Christians," it was first of all *The Imitation of Christ* by Thomas à Kempis that became my constant companion. Then it was the works of John Wesley, and especially his *Journal* and the standard set of his *Sermons*. Then William Law, *A Serious Call to a Devout and Holy Life,* and Jeremy Taylor's *Holy Living and Holy Dying.* Then the various writings of Charles Finney, especially his *Autobiography* and *Revival Lectures.*

As my reading broadened, the writings of Luther and Calvin, along with the later Puritan writers, meant much to me, especially in filling out a theology that could support the spiritual life as one of discipleship and the quest for holiness and power in Christ, without the least touch of perfectionism or meritorious works. (Book 3 of Calvin's *Institutes* has been especially helpful in this regard.) I learned that the follies of discipleshipless "Christianity" and of what Bonhoeffer called "cheap grace" could never be derived from Luther or Calvin.

These great Christian writings meshed closely with the continuous reading of philosophers, from Plato on, which I began upon graduation from high school and continued through two years of life as a migrant agricultural worker. (I carried a volume of Plato in my duffel bag.)

The effect of all my reading has been constantly to bring me back to the Bible, and especially the gospels, and to find in Jesus and his teachings—in what Paul rightly called the "boundless riches of Christ" (Ephesians 3:8)—the wisdom and reality for which human beings vainly strive on their own.

Jesus answers the four great questions of life: What is real? (God and His Kingdom.) Who is well off or "blessed"? (Anyone alive in the Kingdom of God.) Who is a genuinely good person? (Anyone possessed and permeated with agape, God's kind of love.) And how can I become a genuinely good person? (By being a faithful apprentice of

Jesus in Kingdom living, learning from him how to live my life as he would live my life if he were I.)

These are the questions that every human being must answer, because of the very nature of life, and that every great teacher must address. Jesus Christ answers them in the gospels and, then, in his people in a way that becomes increasingly understandable and experimentally verifiable, and as no other person on earth has ever answered them. He evades no question and ducks no issues. The present age is waiting for his disciples to do the same today.

I never cease to be thankful for James Gilchrist Lawson and his little book. It came to me at the right time and helped me to see the actual presence of Jesus Christ and his Kingdom and Spirit in the real life of real people. Thus, it helped me to know something of "what is the hope to which he has called you, what are the riches of his glorious inheritance among the saints, and what is the immeasurable greatness of his power for us who believe, according to the working of his great power. God put this power to work in Christ when he raised him from the dead and seated him at his right hand in the heavenly places" (Ephesians 1:18–20).

Any reader should take from the reading of this book the simple but profound truth that they too can know by experience the truths of Christ and his Kingdom that are set forth in the Bible: that if with all their heart they truly seek God, they will be found and claimed by him (Jeremiah 29:13). This is what human life is for.

CHAPTER 20

A Room of Marvels
by James B. Smith

O F ALL THE TESTS THAT FRAY the confidence and nerves of Christians, the most difficult to bear is undoubtedly the death of loved ones. A legitimate part of the pain is simply *parting*. The fact that I now can no longer pick up the phone and talk to my sister or my father, or visit with them, is a lasting sorrow to me. But the fear and uncertainty in the face of death that is, unfortunately, the rule and not the exception is mainly based in failure of continued life beyond physical death to make any intuitive sense.

As Christians, we know—or at least have heard—the glorious words of Christ and his people about their future life in the presence of God. But frankly, few really believe them. To *really* believe them would be to act straightforwardly and spontaneously as if they were true. It would be to be confident with every pore of our being that any friend of Jesus is far better off dead. It would be to rejoice, in the midst of our parting sorrows, over the indescribably greater well-being of our loved one who has moved on "further up and further into" the greatness of God and His world. Jesus quite reasonably said to his closest friends: "If you loved me, you would rejoice that I am going to the Father, because the Father is greater than I" (John 14:28).

Jesus's attitude toward death is frankly quite cavalier. Here he is himself, dying, and a wretched man dying along with him recognizes him for who he is. He asks Jesus to remember him when he comes into his place of power, his Kingdom. Jesus replies, "You can be sure that this very day you will be with me in Paradise." Now, "Paradise" was understood to be a very good place to be, a place of life and fullness.

This statement goes along with his declaration that those who receive his word will never see, never taste, death (John 8:51–52). That is to say, they will never experience what human beings normally expect is going to happen to them. And again he says at the tomb of Lazarus, "I am the resurrection and the life. Those who believe in me, even though they die, will live, and everyone who lives and believes in me will never die" (John 11:25–26). It was the shared understanding of the Christians of the first generation that Jesus in his person had *destroyed death* (Hebrews 2:14–15; 2 Timothy 1:10).

The central point of reference in all of this is Jesus, who lives on both sides of physical death: his as well as ours. "Because he lives . . . ," the song realistically sings. So Paul, rich in experience of Jesus beyond death, says confidently, "While we are at home in the body we are away from the Lord . . . and we would rather be away from the body and at home with the Lord" (2 Corinthians 5:6–8). He had glimpsed through his own experiences the world where the dying thief had gone to meet Jesus, without benefit of resurrection.

When Paul tells the Philippians that, for him, "living is Christ and dying is gain" (1:21), and that he is "hard pressed between the two: my desire is to depart and be with Christ, for that is far better; but to remain in the flesh is more necessary for you" (1:23–24), he is expressing an unstrained, easy confidence about the continuity of his life and person that was founded on his experiences of the world of God and of the place of Jesus in it. His experiences made it *real for him* and made it easy and natural for him to act as if Jesus and his Kingdom were the enduring reality for the enduring life of those in Jesus's care.

It is assurance of the continuity of our lives under God and in this universe with Him that liberates us from "griev[ing] as others do who have no hope" (1 Thessalonians 4:13). And it is on precisely this point that James Smith's wonderful story helps us. The biblical and theological content is quite solid—though it will be surprising to many who do not put concrete content and image and action into their reading of the Bible and their theological reflection. It must be surprising if it is to address the need. And the need is great—appalling, when you observe how devout Christians suffer in the face of physical death. The reason Jesus wept at the tomb of Lazarus (John 11:35) was certainly because of the misery imposed upon humanity by failure to vividly see the reality of undying life in God—a misery overwhelmingly exemplified in the scene surrounding him at the moment.

It is also important that the treatment be with a light touch—gentle, and slyly humorous. Yet, at the same time, deeply touching, intelligent, and realistic. We are all familiar with this in the writings of C. S. Lewis and a few others. The author here has achieved this fine combination of qualities. As a result, you can enter the writing as you would any outstanding literary work. Enjoy it. Its effects for making real, through imagination, the truth and reality now of life beyond physical death will take care of themselves. The "assurance of the continuity of our lives under God and in this universe with

Him" will creep into your soul. The Word and the Spirit will enter with the story. We will be able to see the truths of scripture in a way that grips us, strengthens us, directs us in life, and lifts the burden of pain and meaninglessness imposed upon those unable to think concretely about the course of their lives as unceasing spiritual beings in God's rich universe. Paradise is now in session.

A PARTING WORD:
"AS YOU GO . . ."

WHAT TO DO NOW! Convert the world? No.

Convert the church? "Judgment," it is famously said, "begins at the house of God." It has the divine light and divine provisions, and because of that is most responsible to guide humankind.

But "no" again. Do not "convert the church."

Your first move "as you go" is, in a manner of speaking: *Convert me*.

If we wish to convert the church and the world, we begin with ourselves. That is something that can, with divine aid, be undertaken with clarity and effectiveness, once we understand discipleship to Jesus and how it works. Our Maestro never told us to convert the world or to reform any religious organizations. He did tell us that, when filled with him, we would bear witness of him "to the ends of the earth" (Acts 1:8). *Witnesses* are those who cause others to *know*. They *wit*-ness. They are not manipulators—no *need* of that—though what they do is radically transformative.

Instead, the Master said, to his *disciples,* "Make disciples." We have no other God-appointed business but this, and we must allow all else to fall away if it will.

So as now "we go," we go *as disciples*. Not as "Christians" in the meanings of that word common today—though that too is fine, so long as we are, first, disciples of Jesus. Never forget that the tiny group to whom Jesus gave his Great Commission were very ordinary people indeed, but people who for about three years had chosen to be with him in the most intimate of fellowships. They watched him live in the manifest presence and action of the Kingdom of God. They received, day by day, the personal influence of his teaching, direction, and correction. They watched him die and knew him beyond death. Perfect they were not, but in his fellowship that was simply not an issue. Everything turned upon what they were learning and who was "Master"-ing them.

My first step then, "as I go," is to *be* his disciple, and constantly to *be learning from him* how to live my life in the Kingdom of God now—my real life, the one I am actually living. Not just in church or on "religious" occasions. That is what he meant by saying, "Seek above all the Kingdom of God *and* his kind of righteousness." (They, of course, are inseparable.) This is his primary directive, and it meets the first need of the ordinary human being wandering about in the world. It is the radical choice: choose your teacher and take your instruction and training. It is the primary act of faith in Jesus for those who have heard him. So long as one neglects or evades this choice, further progress is impossible (Luke 14:26). And, indeed, one is in great danger. One must not play at "faith in Jesus," or at faith in God through him, without having made the radical choice to live as his apprentice. For whatever *that* amounts to will certainly not "work." Which is precisely where we are today, as we discussed in the introduction to this volume. We invent something other than the faith of discipleship, call it "Christianity" perhaps, and then have to live with it.

Once we are disciples with some substance of the Christ-life, the person of Jesus himself, then we are in position to "bear wit-ness," to bring others to know, to bring them to awareness of reality. Then they can learn who *they* are and what God intends for them. They learn how they can become who they should be, who their heart longs to be (if it were only possible!), by counting on Jesus for everything. And they become his apprentices under the care of "his Father and, now, their Father, his God and their God" (John 20:17). The Trinitarian presence enfolds them, along with other disciples (John 14:20–26), and they receive effectual instruction and training on how to do all the things Jesus said. No longer a Great Omission.

Here, then, are the bare bones of what to do now. Step into the Great Commission by practical faith, and the One Really in Charge will see to it that it works, as he always has done when we do that. He is "always with" his disciples, and it is really true that "all things work together for good for those who love God and are inducted into what he is doing" (Romans 8:28). But before we try to cash those checks, notice that they are made out to *disciples of Jesus*.

Well, but, someone says, what about the church and the world? Don't these need to be straightened out? No doubt about that! But it's not your job or mine. And if we undertake on our own to straighten out the church and the world, we will hurt a lot of people and make ourselves miserable. It is God's job, and He will do it, and in the way it should be done—of which we probably have little or no idea at all.

But must we not do *something* about our situation in this world? No doubt we must, and many good opportunities will certainly present themselves to us. Do them the best you can. Just don't take it upon yourself to carry the load, to *make* it happen. Always keep in mind who is really in charge of the greater scene—it isn't you or me. Be humble before others as well as before God—especially before those who are sure we are wrong.

Most important, don't allow your thoughts and efforts to change things to *come before or take the place of your practice of discipleship*, walking with Jesus. That is to be your constant pre-occupation, and what comes of it will wit-ness to and powerfully influence others around you. This is the sure path to changing things, in the church or in the world.

Those who think that the cultivation of inner Christ-likeness through personal discipleship to Jesus amounts to a "privatization" of our faith in him ("quietism" and "pietism" are words often used in that connection) simply do not understand how the spiritual life in Christ works. You *cannot* privatize the fire of God that burns through the life of a disciple of Jesus. This was Jesus's point in saying that "a city built on a hill cannot be hid," and that one does not "light a candle and put it under a bushel" (Matthew 5:14–15; Mark 4:21; Luke 11:33).

This fact has been demonstrated over and over in the history of Christ's people, but never more forcefully than around the Mediterranean world of the second and third centuries A.D. With the force of nothing but the presence of a new life in individuals, spreading from one to another, the world was alarmed at the progress of an unstoppable power in their midst. In his first *Apology*, Tertullian remarks that "men cry out that the state is besieged; the Christians are in the fields, in the ports, in the islands. They mourn, as for a loss, that every sex, age, condition and even rank is going over to this sect."

Origen writes, in *Against Celsus*, that "every form of religion will be destroyed except the religion of Christ, which will alone prevail. And indeed it will one day triumph, as its principles take possession of the minds of men more and more very day."

Tertullian, once again, points out to the surrounding Roman world that "we are but of yesterday, and yet we have filled every place belonging to you—cities, islands, castles, towns, assemblies, your very camps, your tribes, companies, palace, senate, forum; we leave you your temples only. . . . All your ingenious cruelties can accomplish nothing. Our number increases the more you destroy us. The blood of the martyrs is their seed."

All that is needed from us to change things—whether in the church or in the world—is sustained apprenticeship of individuals to Jesus, the Savior of the world so loved by God. Our directions "as we go" are clear: to be disciples—apprentices—of Jesus in Kingdom living and by our life and words as his apprentices to wit-ness, to bring others to know and long for the life that is in us through confidence in him. It's all true. It works. It is accessible to anyone. And there is nothing in the world to compare.

That's all.

NOTES

Chapter 1: Discipleship: For Super Christians Only?

1. *The Cost of Discipleship,* translated by R. H. Fuller (New York: Macmillan, 1963).

2. Leo Tolstoy, *The Kingdom of God and Peace Essays,* translated by Aylmer Maude (Oxford University Press, 1936), p. 158.

Chapter 2: Why Bother with Discipleship?

1. A. W. Tozer, *I Call It Heresy* (Harrisburg, Penn.: Christian Publications, 1974), p. 5f.

Chapter 4: Looking Like Jesus: Divine Resources for a Changed Life Are Always Available

1. See my book *The Spirit of the Disciplines* (Harper & Row, 1988), ch. 1.

Chapter 6: Spiritual Formation in Christ Is for the Whole Life and the Whole Person

1. The central points of this talk are developed at greater length in my *Renovation of the Heart* (NavPress, 2002).

2. See Richard McBrien, *Lives of the Saints* (HarperSanFrancisco, 2001), p. 18ff., for a fine illustration of this.

3. See the diagrams in *Renovation of the Heart,* pp. 38, 40.

4. See my *The Spirit of the Disciplines,* p. 16.

5. *An Augustine Synthesis*, edited by Erich Przywara (Peter Smith Publisher, 1970), p. 89.

Chapter 7: Spiritual Formation in Christ: A Perspective on What It Is and How It Might Be Done

1. Gerald G. May, *Care of Mind, Care of Spirit* (Harper, 1982), p. 6.

2. Marcial Maciel, *Integral Formation of Catholic Priests* (Alba House, 1992).

3. For further discussion of the matters discussed in this article, see my *The Spirit of the Disciplines*.

Chapter 10: Idaho Springs Inquiries Concerning Spiritual Formation

1. See St. John Cassian, *The Monastic Institutes* (London: Saint Austin Press, 1999).

Chapter 11: Personal Soul Care: For Ministers . . . And Others

1. For development of this point, see my *Renovation of the Heart*, especially chapter 2.

2. For some illustrations of how this works, see Frank Laubach, "Letters of a Modern Mystic" and "Game with Minutes," in *Frank C. Laubach: Man of Prayer* (Laubach Literacy International/New Readers Press, 1990).

3. Thomas Watson, *All Things for Good* (1663; reprint, Banner of Truth Trust, 1986), 74.

4. Quoted in Dallas Willard, *The Spirit of the Disciplines* (San Francisco: Harper & Row, 1988), 165.

5. For further discussion, see Richard Foster, *Celebration of Discipline* (Harper & Row, 1978), as well as his *Streams of Living Water* (HarperSanFrancisco, 1998). See also my *The Spirit of the Disciplines*.

6. See Foster, *Celebration of Discipline*, as well as chapter 9 of my *The Spirit of the Disciplines*, for ways of listing and classifying many of the disciplines and for discussions of particular ones.

Chapter 12: Spiritual Disciplines, Spiritual Formation, and the Restoration of the Soul

1. This condition is described in detail in my *The Divine Conspiracy*, chapter 2.

2. On the amazing current revival of interest in the soul, see M. Ventura, "Soul in the Raw: America Can Sell Anything, Including That Most Ephemeral Commodity: The Soul," *Psychology Today* 30, no. 3 (1997): 58–83.

3. Major historical figures in this tradition are Plato (*Republic*), Aristotle (*On the Soul* and *Nicomachean Ethics*), and Plotinus (*Enneads,* especially the fourth "Ennead"); their writings have appeared in many editions. In the Christian tradition, Tertullian wrote his own *On the Soul,* available in the Fathers of the Church series (Washington, D.C.: Catholic University of America Press, 1950). There are numerous works by St. Augustine on the nature of the soul. About the same time as Augustine, Nemesius, Bishop of Emesa, wrote his *On the Nature of Man,* which is largely a treatment of the soul (available in volume 4 of the Library of Christian Classics [Philadelphia: Westminster Press, 1955]). The classical treatment from the Christian point of view is still St. Thomas Aquinas, "Treatise on Man," in his *Summa Theologica,* part 1, questions 75–90 (many editions).

4. Plato, *Laws,* book 10.

5. Aristotle, *Nicomachean Ethics,* book 2.

6. For extensive treatment of the spiritual disciplines, see Foster, *Celebration of Discipline.* See also my *The Spirit of the Disciplines* and *Renovation of the Heart.*

Chapter 15: Jesus the Logician

1. See my "Degradation of Logical Form," *Axiomathes* 1–3 (1997): 1–22, esp. 3–7.

2. Herbert Welch, ed., *Selections from the Writings of the Rev. John Wesley* (Eaton & Mains, 1901), p. 186.

3. Welch, *Selections from the Writings of the Rev. John Wesley,* p. 198.

4. For necessary elaboration of many themes touched upon in this paper, see J. P. Moreland's crucial book *Love Your God with All Your Mind* (NavPress, 1997).

Chapter 19: When God Moves In: My Experience with *Deeper Experiences of Famous Christians*

1. James Gilchrist Lawson, *Deeper Experiences of Famous Christians* (Barbour Publishing, 2000), p. 133.

CREDITS AND PERMISSIONS

Chapter 1: Discipleship: For Super Christians Only?

Originally published in *Christianity Today* (October 10, 1980). Also published as Appendix II in *The Spirit of the Disciplines* (HarperSanFrancisco, 1988).

Chapter 2: Why Bother with Discipleship?

Originally published in an occasional publication, *The Journey* (1995), for a Biola University conference on spiritual transformation.

Chapter 3: Who Is Your Teacher?

First published in *Promise*, a Korean Christian publication of Tyrannus International Ministry, January 1996.

Chapter 4: Looking Like Jesus: Divine Resources for a Changed Life Are Always Available

Originally published in *Christianity Today* (August 20, 1990).

Chapter 5: The Keys to the Keys to the Kingdom

A shorter version of this piece appeared in *Leadership Journal* 19, no. 4 (Fall 1998): 57.

Chapter 6: Spiritual Formation in Christ Is for the Whole Life and the Whole Person

An address for a conference at Samford University (Beeson Divinity School), Birmingham, Alabama (October 2-4, 2000), later published in the conference proceedings, *For All the Saints: Evangelical Theology and Christian Spirituality*, edited by Timothy George and Alister McGrath (Westminster John Knox Press, 2003), pp. 39–53. Used by permission.

Chapter 7: Spiritual Formation in Christ: A Perspective on What It Is and How It Might Be Done

These remarks, prepared for a seminar in conjunction with the inauguration of Richard Mouw as president of Fuller Theological Seminary on October 22, 1993, were published in *Journal of Psychology and Theology*, vol. 28, no. 4, © 2000, Rosemead School of Psychology, Biola University: 254–58.

Chapter 8: The Spirit Is Willing, But ... The Body as a Tool for Spiritual Growth

First published in *The Christian Educator's Handbook on Spiritual Formation*, edited by Kenneth Gangel and James Wilhoit, Baker Academic, a division of Baker Publishing Group, 1998.

Chapter 9: Living in the Vision of God

A booklet first published by Tell the Word, a publishing ministry associated with the Church of the Saviour, Washington, D.C., 2003.

Chapter 10: Idaho Springs Inquiries Concerning Spiritual Formation

Previously unpublished. In the fall of 1999 a small group of Christian teachers gathered in retreat near Idaho Springs, Colorado, to prayerfully reflect on the meaning and prospects of Christian spiritual formation today.

Chapter 11: Personal Soul Care: For Ministers ... And Others

First published in *The Pastor's Guide to Effective Ministry*, edited by William H. Willimon, Beacon Hill Press, 2002.

Chapter 12: Spiritual Disciplines, Spiritual Formation, and the Restoration of the Soul

First published in *Journal of Psychology and Theology*, vol. 26, no. 1, © 1998, Rosemead School of Psychology, Biola University.

Chapter 13: Christ-Centered Piety: The Heart of the Evangelical

This is a considerably revised version of a talk given at Harvard Divinity School at the inaugural conference of the Alonzo L. McDonald Family Professorship in Evangelical Theological Studies in 1998. It first appeared in the conference volume *Where Shall My Wond'ring Soul Begin?: The Landscape of Evangelical Piety and Thought*, edited by Mark A. Knoll and Ronald F. Thiemann, © 2000, Wm. B. Eerdmans Publishing Co., Grand Rapids MI. Reprinted by permission of the publisher; all rights reserved.

Chapter 14: Why?

Originally published in *World Christian/U* (January 1989), a magazine for university and college students.

Chapter 15: Jesus the Logician

First published in *Christian Scholar's Review,* vol. 28, no. 4, 1999.

Chapter 16: *Letters by a Modern Mystic* by Frank C. Laubach

From *Christian Spirituality,* edited by Frank Magill and Ian McGreat, Harper and Row, 1998.

Chapter 17: *The Interior Castle* of Teresa of Avila

Originally published in *Teresa of Avila: Selections from* The Interior Castle (Harper-SanFrancisco, 2004).

Chapter 18: *Invitation to Solitude and Silence* by Ruth Haley Barton

Taken from *Invitation to Solitude and Silence* by Ruth Haley Barton. © 2004 by Ruth Haley Barton. Used with permission of InterVarsity Press, P.O. Box 1400, Downers Grove, IL 60515. www.ivpress.com.

Chapter 19: When God Moves In: My Experience with *Deeper Experiences of Famous Christians*

Originally published in *Indelible Ink,* edited by Scott Larsen (WaterBrook Press, 2003).

Chapter 20: *A Room of Marvels* by James B. Smith

First published as the Afterword in *A Room of Marvels* by James Bryan Smith (Broadman Holman, 2004).